THE ART OF
HEALING

THE ART OF HEALING

A JOURNEY INTO THE MIRACULOUS

JOSH KLINKENBERG

InFlame
Publishing House

Published by:
  InFlame Publishing House
  Tauranga, New Zealand
  www.inflameministries.com
  info@inflameministries.com

Cover by Paul Wayland Lee, www.leewaycreative.com
Editing, layout and interior design: Carol Cantrell

Dedication

This book is dedicated to my son, Elijah Joshua Klinkenberg. You are a hero of mine. Thank you for your patience, kindness, and perseverance. Your life has taught me more than I ever knew possible. At the time I finished writing this book, you just turned six. This is for your children's children. May we, as a family, forever know the increasing greatness of our God!

I love you, son.

One generation shall praise Your works to another, and shall declare Your mighty acts.

Psalm 145:4

Acknowledgement

I'd like to give a special thanks to my wife Amberley. You have sacrificed so much to see a dream in my heart become a reality. The way you love and encourage both me and our kids has taught me what His love really looks like. Though our journey has not been easy, sharing it with you has made it fun!

Thanks, my love! I love you!

Endorsements

If there is someone who understands enduring prayers and unwavering faith, it is my friend Josh Klinkenberg. I have had the honor of knowing Josh, his wife Amberley, and their beautiful children for 5 years. I have always been so encouraged by the way they contend for more of God and champion those around them to do the same. I have watched them wrestle for their breakthroughs and have witnessed the miracles of God in their lives.

Josh's book, *The Art Of Healing*, is a challenge to us all to walk in the destiny Jesus paid for. This book inspires me to press in for more healing!

—Kim Walker-Smith
President, Jesus Culture Music and Jesus Culture Publishing

I would like to fully recommend to you Josh Klinkenberg's book, *The Art Of Healing*. This is not just a "how to" book on healing; it is a practical guide on how to cultivate true faith for healing in your life. As you read this book, there is an amazing impartation of the compassionate heart of Jesus that is sure to unlock the fullness of God's healing power in your life. I love both the practical and spiritual wisdom that Josh brings to the reader through his and Amberley's walk and journey with God in life.

In this book you will be challenged to look beyond the natural and into the supernatural realm of God's love and power. This book is a must-read for those who are contending to receive healing and breakthrough from Jesus.

—Jerame Nelson
Living At His Feet Ministries
Author of *Encountering Angels, Burning Ones,* and *Manifesting God's Love Through Signs, Wonders, & Miracles*

I have had the privilege and joy of journeying this life with Josh side-by-side. I have known and loved him for 13 years, and in all that time, he has hungered for the full and true gospel. Even in the hardest time of both of our lives with our son, Josh continued to long for truth. His faith and courage is what has held our family together through thick and thin. Josh's loyalty and love for Jesus are inspiring to me; his faith has become unshakable, encouraging, and challenging to me as well. I get to experience firsthand his love and humility on a daily basis. I am so thankful to God for him—for the husband he is, and the amazing father he is and longs to be

I have watched him write this book over the last 5 years; it truly has come out of a long journey of relationship and communion with Jesus. I watched Josh pour his whole heart into writing *The Art Of Healing* and you will see that not only does it have amazing revelation of Scripture, but also revelation from his journey—crying out and believing for our own son. Josh tackles some hard questions in this book; these are all questions he has sought the Lord for the answers to over the years.

I know *The Art Of Healing* will encourage others battling with long-term illness and disabilities as well as those who simply have a hunger to heal the sick. This book will encourage you to step out more and believe in God for healing. The activations Josh included here will both inspire and challenge your mindset. You will be taken on your own personal journey of discovering the fullness of the Kingdom of God. Josh has a heart to see sons and daughters in New Zealand—and all over the world—step into *all* that God has given us.

I believe this book is going to act as a tool for God to pour out His fullness on the earth. As you read *The Art Of Healing*, I pray that you will have an increased desire for the supernatural and a greater level of faith in God for complete healing for your loved ones and for all those you come across in your life.

—Amberley Klinkenberg
Wife and best friend
Co-Founder and Director of InFlame Ministries

This book is a living revelation that has been beaten into steadfast reality in Josh's heart, mind, and life on the anvil of incredible hardship. Josh and Amberley have journeyed a road full of temptation to doubt God's goodness, yet they have journeyed it in a way that has left them concretely convinced that He is good.

In *The Art Of Healing*, Josh engages many of the tough questions regarding healing and the nature of God and he does so in the most real, thoughtful, and living way.

The contents of these pages are gold refined in fire; they are laced with life, hope, sincerity, inspiration, and the reality of God.

—Matt Lansdowne
Senior Associate Leader
Bethel Church Whangarei, New Zealand

In *The Art Of Healing*, Josh doesn't just talk Scriptures and theological ideas . . . he lives it. The marriage between the divine, the inspired Word of God, the art of personal testimony, and the day-to-day of a life challenged to walk out of the bondage of sickness and disease is so evident in this book.

If you think you know all there is to know about healing, think again. I found myself having many 'light bulb' moments reading this book. Understanding healing is like peeling off the layers of an onion: learning and understanding more the deeper you go. That's exactly what this book is like—taking off layers to reveal deep hidden truths.

Yet, I love the tension of the challenge of believing in the midst of Josh and Amberley's personal experience. Theirs is not a perfect story, but it's a real one. Theirs is a story with many answers, but also many confronting questions, and in the midst of it all, a deep faith and trust in Jesus.

You can read this book knowing they have had challenges in the arena of healing on a daily basis yet they are seeing God move in powerful miraculous ways! I believe their story will echo through the halls of history and be marked as one that is part of a new emerging healing move of God. I highly recommend reading this powerful book. It will change your perspective and release healing in your own life.

—Roma Waterman
Award-winning singer/songwriter/author
Director Sounds of the Nations Oceania

———

Growing up in a Bible-believing home, there were many things that Jesus said that I believed *could* happen, but being honest with myself, I didn't believe *would* happen. Healing was one of those 'mysterious ways' of God that seemed to touch the random few yet was subject to God's 'whims'. Even today, being immersed in an ever-increasing culture of healing miracles, I believe there are many who have yet to fully realise how to walk out this promised gift of healing.

Without a doubt, *The Art Of Healing* is a powerfully unique book that will have a radical life-changing affect on those who are hungry to walk out the promises of God, particularly in healing. Josh does a wonderful job of building our faith by revealing the Father's heart for healing as well as hitting those hard questions we all have when we don't see the 'results' we want. And yet, Josh is not satisfied to just give you his revelations about healing, which in themselves are full of spiritual depth, humor and vulnerability. Because he is an equipper, Josh activates you, building your faith one step at a time until it is tangibly evident and you are consistently witnessing the Father's heart being released through you.

This book is a life-changer, and I do not say this lightly. I believe with my whole heart that through this book, those longing to walk as Jesus walked will be taught, encouraged, and more importantly, activated in seeing the gift of healing manifested through their own life.

—Bethany Hicks
Sounds of the Nations North American Director
Founder and Director of The Greenhouse Culture

———

In this book, *The Art Of Healing*, Josh shares from his own life journey his passion to know the fullness of everything Jesus made available on the cross—to know it experientially, not just theoretically! Having had a desire to experience and share the healing power of Jesus early on in his life, Josh brings us along the road that Jesus has led him on since then, allowing us, with refreshing transparency, to see the highs and lows, the triumphs and setbacks, the joys and sorrows that he and Amberley have experienced. Both his personal encounters with Jesus and his understanding of biblical truth have fashioned a strong foundation and perspective that, while having been sorely tested, has not weakened, but rather has grown stronger. Josh has been confronted with many of the beliefs held by others that would try and convince him to settle for less than everything Jesus promised and made available. With boldness, and yet also with humility, he dismantles those beliefs and arguments, showing clearly from Scripture the full inheritance that is available to us today if we will position ourselves in trust and faith, laying hold of the power and authority that has been made available to us.

This book is not one with slick formulas, trite platitudes and untested theory. It has been fashioned in a journey of personal suffering through the sickness of Josh and Amberley's son, Elijah, and will be a huge encouragement to all, especially to those who find themselves standing in adverse circumstances, contending for the full expression of "Your Kingdom come, Your will be done on earth as it is in heaven." *The Art Of Healing* is an invaluable workbook for those of us who know that there is more than what we are currently experiencing in healing and in other expressions of Kingdom reality. It gives clear and simple assignments that we can put into practice to grow in our ability to be agents of healing and change in the lives of others. Get ready to be encouraged, inspired and challenged!

—Rob Packer
Team Leader, XP Ministries, New Zealand

Contents

Foreword

I grew up in a church environment that did not embrace the power of God as a present reality. In essence, my church believed that the gospel was only about what God had done in the past and would do in the future—not about what He was doing now. Everything miraculous in Scripture, including the passages that mentioned or depicted the healing power of God, was either skipped over or referenced in a list of experiences that were no longer available for believers.

Then, when I was 19 years old, Bill Johnson became my pastor, and introduced the gospel to me in an entirely new way. Rather than emphasizing that the gospel gives us the hope of heaven after death, Bill taught that

17

heaven is eternally present and breaking into our reality in powerful, redemptive ways. He explained that Jesus' miracles were not merely signs of His divinity, but actually demonstrated God's will for people to experience the full restoration of their bodies, souls, and spirits through the finished work of the cross—both in this present life and in the one to come.

I ended up serving on staff at Bill's church for eighteen years. Living in a community of people who believed it was God's will to heal, and that He still healed today, changed everything about how I experienced the gospel. I was swept into a corporate quest to know the heart of the Father and demonstrate His power to a lost and dying world. Along the way, our community witnessed many who were healed by the power of God. We also saw people who were not healed. However, though we wrestled with the unanswered question of why some were healed and others weren't, especially when those we had contended for passed away, we ultimately settled the issue of healing in our hearts. We refused to define our theology by our experience, good or bad, and insisted that our beliefs align with what we read in the Word. Returning again and again to the model and teaching of Jesus, we affirmed that sickness was not from God, that it was His will to heal, and that His healing power is available today. We would not settle for pursuing anything less.

As I read *The Art Of Healing*, by my friend, Josh Klinkenberg, I was again wonderfully provoked by the question, "What are you willing to settle for?" Even after eighteen years of believing in, pursuing, and witnessing the power of God to heal and restore people, I still need to be confronted by this simple question—and so do you. Will you believe God and pursue the fullness of what He has made available through the cross, or will you settle for less? Josh has written a book that will challenge you to settle for nothing less than embracing all that Jesus paid for and daily experiencing His life and power. In the pages ahead, he invites you to walk more closely with Jesus, the Healer—to become intimate with the One who bore every sickness on the cross. He does not call you to strive more, but to rest in what God has already accomplished. Neither does he promise that you can have all the answers this side of heaven, but assures no matter what happens, you can have Him.

I am so grateful that Josh is calling the Church to believe God for healing, and to step into a life that sees healing regularly. My heart longs for believers of every denomination and theological background to gain a deeper understanding—not just intellectually, but experientially—of all that the cross has accomplished, and taste the fullness of the miracle-working power of God. Thankfully, I have seen many parts of the Church begin to believe that God heals today. However, there is still a gap between believing He heals and seeing it as a normal part of the Christian life. Josh works to bridge that gap by tackling the thought processes that hinder the flow of God's power in your life, and empowering you with the theological and practical foundation necessary to see Jesus, the Healer, moving powerfully in and through you. I, therefore, urge you to embark on reading this book with an open heart, hungry and expectant to learn how to join Jesus in practicing the art of healing.

—Banning Liebscher
Director of Jesus Culture
Author of *Jesus Culture, Journey Of A World Changer*, and
Spiritual Java

Foreword

One of my mentors used to say, "I don't trust a man who doesn't walk with a limp." Please understand this particular mentor was given to a gift for mystical statements made without offering any real explanations. I would then take these cryptic statements (as he surely intended) and process them over time to find amazing nuggets of wisdom. This particular gem of "walking with a limp" is, of course, a reference to Jacob wrestling all night with God and coming away with a new name, a new heart, and a physical limp. Metaphorically, it means that people are more trustworthy who have had to wrestle with God for the blessings they carry.

Josh is one of those trustworthy men that "walks with

a limp." He has wrestled through a long, dark night with God and come away wise beyond his years and eternally impacted by his encounters. History tells us that it's not your greatest victories that ultimately define you, but it is what you do and how you respond in the midst of your greatest battles. True champions, like Josh and Amberley, have learned to turn their valley of troubles into a door of hope.

It is for these reasons that I would describe this book, *The Art Of Healing*, as "trench art." During World War I, soldiers waiting in the battle trenches would use their time to craft empty shell casings into beautiful works of art. Trench art "offers an insight not only to their feelings and emotions about the war, but also their surroundings and the materials they had available to them" (Wikipedia). These pages are thick with a solid theology of healing, hammered out on the anvil of real life experiences, but with a beauty of faith and vulnerability that is truly art.

One of the things I most love about this book is the cry for reformers to step in the gap and contend for breakthroughs in healing beyond the measure of what we've seen. Josh shows us both sides of the coin, reminding us that Christ has done His part for our total healing, but challenging us to consider what we will do with what God has given us.

This generation has seen some of the greatest healings in church history, but there is still so much more for us to take hold of. *The Art Of Healing* presents a launching pad for the more of God our hearts are crying for.

—Dan McCollam
Leader, The Mission Church, Vacaville, California
Founder of Sounds of the Nations
Author of several books including *God Vibrations*

I am Your canvas
You are the brush
Changing me
Oh such love
As You paint my life
Into a masterpiece
Each day a new colour
Each moment a song
An anthem of love
Composed on Your cross
I know You've been here
Waiting for me
To come sing along[1]

Introduction

The Art Of Healing: A Journey Into The Miraculous is a book I have written over the last several years. I felt it necessary to write what the Lord has shown my wife and I as we have walked with Him through a journey that has challenged everything I know about God's nature as the Healer. I have heard a lot of opinions about God and His will to heal over the years, but not many of them come from those who are in the centre of the storm. So I decided to record the things that we have learned along the way—those treasures of the darkness we had the privilege of digging up. We have encountered God's heart for His children in such a way that we just could not keep it to ourselves.

The purpose of this book is to give a better

understanding of God's heart on matters that are often so misunderstood, or simply ignored, because certain situations make no sense whatsoever. My goal is that we would be enabled to "settle" our faith in God so that we might walk in the fullness of the power and life that Jesus promised us.

There are so many contending opinions these days about divine healing, especially within the body of Christ. Because of this, to be "settled" in our faith in God and to simply believe is not as easy as one would hope. Our trust and faith in Him must be steady and sure. James put it like this:

> *For the one who doubts is like the surf of the sea, driven and tossed by the wind. For that man ought not to expect that he will receive anything from the Lord.*
>
> James 1:6-7

To be settled in your heart enables you to ask of the Lord with a faith that attracts answers. As we know, the devil comes to steal, kill, and destroy; but Jesus came that we "would have life, and *have it to the full!*"[2] My aim with this book is to serve that very intention: to partner with Jesus' desire for the fullness of God and His kingdom in you!

I have included an activation and/or reflection section at the end of each chapter. Here I challenge you further in your own wonderful adventure with Holy Spirit and the gift of healing. I believe you will find these exercises fun and exciting as you respond to His leading and see the results.

There are times in this book where I am fairly blunt and forthright as I explore a number of commonly-held opinions in the church today. Although I won't apologise for this, it is worth mentioning that as you read through chapter by chapter, you will come to understand why I am so direct on certain issues. The statements I make about sickness and suffering are by no means done so lightly. This is something that is extremely close to our hearts. We are only able to speak about such things from a place of deep reverence and an awareness of God's goodness.

Some may wonder, "What qualifies a young man such as yourself to write a book about healing?" The answer is hidden in our personal journey and the road that we have been walking the last number of years. The strength of our faith did not come about by going to conferences or the most popular ministry schools, as wonderful as those are. Rather, our faith has been picked up piece by piece along a road that led us through intense fire where we have been tested and tried to our limits.

My objective is not an attempt to simply pen a few good theological arguments. Our story has taken shape in the "trenches" of the battlefield with many gut-wrenching lows and joy-filled highs. This battle that we were drafted into was not one we took by choice, but we chose it because of love. As our journey unfolds in the following chapters, you will see that we were not fighting for the lives of others, but rather, we were contending for the life of our own son.

I have made careful choices as I wrote this book to only include that which has been tried and tested in my own personal life. Because of this I can say that what I share here is more than just opinion; it is my life and my daily practice.

I pray that as you read this book, you are encouraged to take up the fullness of the life that the Father has given to you in Christ—a life of raw power, reckless love, overwhelming joy, perfect peace, and absolute authority.

You have made them to be a kingdom and priests to our God; and they will reign upon the earth.

Revelation 5:10

End Notes

1. Song, "I Love You", written by Josh Klinkenberg, copyright © 2013 Jesus Culture Music, administered exclusively by Capitol CMP Lyrics. Printed with permission. All rights reserved. International copyright secured.

2. John 10:10, NIV.

My love is awakened
My heart is on fire
Now I'm Yours
You are mine
Our life together
Is Heaven's love song
I'll follow Your lead
As we dance
Through this life
Till storms are still
And dark is light
As You take my hand
I come alive
And my heart
Begins to sing

"I Love You"
by Josh Klinkenberg

1

A Morning Like Any

Other

I
t is a morning just like any other . . . a typical morning that for most people means another day of work, university or school. But for a few, it is another day of exhausting effort and ever-increasing uncertainty.

As I write this, I am sitting at a special-needs school for children. I am observing parents as they walk their children in from the car park with a silent, sobering understanding that this could be the last day they spend with their beloved child. These parents understand that the next moment, even, could be their very last. There is a common look among those who live with such incredible stress and brokenness. You can see it when you look past the observable tiredness. It is the look of hopelessness and helplessness. It is a look that scares me—a look that keeps me awake at night and haunts me to take action. To know that people live day-to-day with an anticipated sense of, "This is it!"—the ongoing, foreboding feeling that the rest of life will be spent in a kind of personal hell made up of unachievable demands that continually require every bit of mental, physical, and emotional strength that can be mustered up, and then some. Although this same "look" is clearly evident in the eyes of many people we are in contact with every day, I see it especially in the eyes of this one group in particular—the parents of special-needs children. I see it in the eyes of these parents all over the country that engage in this same activity—dropping their precious little gems of love and beauty off at school. But it is not just any school; it is a *special* school. These parents hold on to a desperate hope that this special-needs school will miraculously be able to teach their beautiful ones the ability to communicate in some way—any way!— even if only for the slightest moment. Just something. . . anything.

The living situation of these particular parents is not something they would wish upon their worst enemy.

My attention is drawn to a mother leading her young boy to the door of his classroom. Somehow she managed to achieve a half a smile as the teacher warmly welcomed her son inside. That was all she could do in that moment. Clearly this young mother had just spent every bit of willpower she had left to manage a smile that didn't really seem worth the effort. It seemed as if every muscle in her body was drained attempting to achieve what for most people is an unconscious greeting done out of habit.

I cannot help but wonder what the scene would look like if Jesus took a walk through this little school: lives would be changed, freedom would be released, those parents, filled with heartache and imprisoned in hopelessness, would be instantly set free and filled with joy! The only thing that this situation could possibly be likened to would be switching a floodlight on in a pitch-black room, transforming a place of complete darkness into a place of extreme brilliance—so bright that it hurts the eyes!

Then I consider the fact that we are to be "as He is in this world." Selah. Oh, to see that "look" on the faces of these parents dissolve at the sight of the One they have been longing for unknowingly all their life. I long to see that haunting look of hopelessness destroyed under the weight of Love Himself as He fills them with life and hope by answering the deepest cry of their hearts—the healing of their young ones.

Looking at this kind of raw hardship causes a pain to flood my heart that could be dealt with in one of two ways. The first is to give in to the temptation to pin this on God. If I choose to believe that this hardship is God's doing, then it removes from me any demand for change to take place. This first way is by far the easiest as it provides a "way out" of the pain without taking any responsibility to make a difference.

But when I see that "look" in the eyes of the parents—that haunting, hopeless look—and experience firsthand the struggles these children face every day, I am forced to find another way! Rather than attempting to remove the pain from my heart, I allow it to stir me to a place of deep compassion—the kind of compassion that moved Jesus to take action. I know that this "look" that so haunts me is not one that is seen in the face of Jesus. Therefore, the pain of seeing these beloved people live like this must be eased in only one way: love!—by the love that brings wholeness in spirit, soul, and body.

The Art of Healing

Their suffering must be dealt with in a way that does not allow us to be "okay" with their pain. To resign ourselves to a position that leaves people in their state of suffering is animalistic at best. And yet, even animals seem to care for their own. Selah.

There must be an answer to the problem of suffering that does not use "God's will" as the commonly-held scapegoat just so we can sleep peacefully at night. The truth is, the only way this pain in my heart could possibly be dealt with would be to see these situations of injustice changed for good. We must stop treating people with spiritual "band-aids" that only serve to cover up a wound rather than completely heal it. We only use these spiritual "band-aids" because we have submitted to the lie that we are powerless to bring breakthrough and change.

I have come to realise a number of important things on this journey into the unknown. One is that to hide from the pain of someone else's situation simply makes you useless to them. It is like taking a sedative when the world needs you to wake up! We are in a love war, and to separate yourself from someone's hardship in order to keep your own heart comfortable is to withhold the very love that ultimately wins the war. The reality is, compassion moved Jesus into action. He never hid Himself from the pain of another. And at the same time, He never allowed Himself to fall prey to the temptation of powerlessness. When compassion moved Him, people were healed and delivered from all that was out of alignment with heaven.

To feel such intense heartache of other people's suffering is to truly be alive. But to know that we carry something, or rather Someone, who cures all, is what makes us unique.

At times we are guilty of unconsciously creating excuses that allow a destructive situation to remain

34

unchanged simply because we feel powerless to change it. Out of this feeling of powerlessness we feel compelled to create some sort of logical explanation as to why this situation has happened. We come up with excuses that remove any personal responsibility to be the agent of change we were created, anointed, and commissioned to be. We tell ourselves, "They don't have faith for healing," or, "God is teaching them about the sufferings of Christ." Both of these explanations fail to acknowledge the biblical fact that God has given us both power and authority to release His goodness in every situation. It is time we take responsibility, not only for the suffering in the world, but for the power and authority that He has given us to remove it!

I am tired of sympathising with people in powerless pity. I am tired of listening to Christians who carry the very presence of the Living God but pray powerless prayers that produce no effect on someone's day-to-day reality. Aren't you? I am tired of a church that runs from the spotlight found in the worlds' hardship—a spotlight that is destined to shine its brightest in the darkness. I long to be more and more like Peter and John who caught the gaze of the man lame from birth, and declared to him with commanding faith, "Look at us!"

People do not need to be medicated with a nice Bible verse to quote. What they need is the reality of the Living God. I long to be a part of a people who stare right into the eyes of the "giants" of this world and say, "Look at me!" Not out of a need to be seen, but out of an awareness that we carry the very answers to the world's problems. It is time we begin to stand in all that we truly are, looking at the "mountains" of the world and fearlessly declaring, "Look at us! We might not have worldly riches, but what we do have, we give to you. Now get up and walk!"

As I sit here at this special-needs school this morning, surrounded by children who were born with the most challenging of limitations, I am stirred more than ever in this life of healing that we, the church, have been given. It is a welcomed wake-up call to sit and witness families who, contrary to the opinions of many, are not being drawn closer to God because of their extreme suffering. Rather, they live in a place of despair where having given up all hope, they are overshadowed by a continual feeling that they are slowly drowning.

Many of them have already surrendered to the lie that "this is just their lot" and nothing can be done about it. Like Peter, they would grab on for dear life if someone would just come and reach out a hand of hope to keep them from sinking into despair. To change their situation would be to remove the overwhelming stranglehold on their soul that leaves them with a feeling of being slowly suffocated to the point where every breath becomes harder—more trouble than it's worth.

Most people who retire to a belief that God allows—or even gives—this kind of suffering, would do themselves and everyone around them a huge favour if they would get involved with a family who is dealing with such life conditions. Get in amidst the incredible pain that is an everyday part of life for people who have seriously disabled children. Get in amidst the sleepless nights and daily frustrations these families deal with. Get to a place where you so love these children that your heart aches to see them truly enjoy life as they should, instead of the way they have to endure their painful difficulties and persevere through them. Get so filled with love, that like the parents of these kids, you long for them to respond, even if only for a second to show that they recognise you; where you long to hear them simply say a word—one word, any word!—just to demonstrate one simple sign of life! When you have lived in this way, then I will listen to your view of God's heart for these children.

It really hurts to hear people coming up with an "opinion" of God's heart when they are not actively involved in the area they have developed an opinion about! It is these types of opinions that can cause our heart to become callused and hardened towards those in need around us. A person with this kind of heart can simply walk away and feel nothing for the hurting person. But this is not the heart of Jesus or how He lived on the earth.

If your opinion can exist outside of the deep compassion that Jesus lived with—compassion that moved Him to the point where He *had* to take action—then it's safe to say that opinion is wrong.

Have you ever noticed that Jesus calmed the storm from the centre of it? He walked right into the middle of one storm while He slept through the middle of another. But the fact remains the same: Jesus calmed the storm from the centre. So often we look at storms from the outskirts, too afraid to get near them. And because we feel helpless to do anything about it, we develop an explanation that says, "God did it," which gives us some sort of peace to leave the people in the centre of their storm of suffering as we look the other way. Jesus walked straight into the middle of that storm knowing He had full authority over it. I believe it is time we start to walk head-on into the storms that we see others sinking and drowning in and release peace through the authority He gave to us!

You might be wondering what I am doing sitting at a special-needs school for children in the first place. It is because one of the students here is my son. At the time of this writing, my son, Elijah, is six-years old.

REFLECTION

Take a moment to reflect upon your own current heart condition. When the topic of healing is spoken about, what do you feel inside? Are you excited, interested, hungry to learn, filled with a sense of wonder? If so, that's great! Steward that hunger and passion well so that you can get all that God has for you in this season.

If you don't identify with the feelings above, that too is absolutely fine. What we then need to ask ourselves is, "How do I feel?" Do you feel anxious, irritated, uneasy, annoyed, or frustrated? All of these are valid feelings that we often try to ignore. If you can identify that you are feeling a "check" in your heart towards the subject of healing, the key is to ask the Father, "Why?"

You do not, in any way, need to hide those feelings. Know that God has already seen them all along anyway, and the cool thing is, they don't bother Him one bit! He knows the reason you feel that way and it is important to know that how you are feeling can often come from a place in your heart that God wants to breath upon.

If this is you, take a moment and ask the Father these two questions:

- Why do I feel this way?

- What happened in my life that has caused me to have a hesitation towards this aspect of You?

What did He show you in response?

If you feel to, ask His forgiveness for holding that thing in your heart. Ask the Holy Spirit to help you, lead you, and walk with you into the depths of the Father's heart to heal.

Lastly, answer these two simple questions:

- In regards to God's will to heal, what opinions do you hold in your heart, both the good and the bad?

- Are you willing to put these opinions to the test?

Both, right or wrong opinions remain opinions when they are untested. It's important that we can identify which truths we believe that are still untested in our lives. Remember, to biblically "know" something is to intimately experience it.

When the truth of His Word is able to be demonstrated in power through us, then we have something to offer the world around us.

Death is defeated
The grave has not won
'Twas man's King
God's only Son
His radiant beauty
May we become
The glorious saving
Of man has begun

"Hymn of Redemption"
by Josh Klinkenberg

2

We Need the Gift

of Healing

The world already has it in their minds that God likes to see people suffer. With this understanding, pagan religions that endorse beliefs like "karma" seem to try to make sense of the suffering world. In many religions and belief systems, suffering is permissible because "people are getting what they deserve." If we, as the church, preach this same message, then we are no different than other earthly religions. The thing that sets us apart, however, is that our God is good and He desires to reveal His goodness through His people. He is not interested in giving people what they deserve, but rather, what He paid for! The fact is, our God does not take delight in suffering like other gods do. Our God takes great pleasure in restoring those who are suffering with healing and wholeness. He is a God who delights in His children, loves to make their dreams a reality, and all while destroying the evil works of the enemy. He is a God of blessing, joy, and abundance, not just in thought, but in reality.

Our God's name is Healer, and healing is a normal part of His kingdom. It is, therefore, a gift that all believers can—and should—move freely in. I say it is a "normal" part of the Kingdom because every time Jesus told His disciples to preach or proclaim the Kingdom, He followed it with a command to "heal the sick." In 1 Corinthians 12:30 we see that there is a "gift of healing" which is given to some, but not to all. However, this does not mean that the ability to receive and release healing is not for every believer.

From this same chapter we also know that not all are prophets, and yet everyone is able to prophesy. In fact, Paul goes on to tell us:

Pursue love, yet desire earnestly spiritual gifts, but especially that you may prophesy.

1 Corinthians 14:1

In regards to this spiritual gift, Paul encourages us to "desire . . . that you may prophesy." So, although not all believers are prophets, all can prophesy. There is a big difference. In the same way, although not all may have the gift of healing, all can heal the sick. Jesus did not differentiate between His disciples by pointing to each one saying, "You have the gift of healing so you heal the sick; you don't. You have a gift of prophecy so you should prophesy." He just commanded them all to heal the sick.

So it is with us. What Paul is addressing in these chapters concerns church leadership and order at corporate gatherings. It would be wrong to take these recommendations that Paul makes in 1 Corinthians 12 and 14 and apply them exclusively to missions and evangelism. In doing so, you would actually be contradicting the very thing Jesus commissioned all of us to do: preach the Kingdom by healing the sick, cast out demons, cleanse lepers, and raise the dead.[1]

The ability to see the sick healed is not determined by a gift one has or does not have. What qualifies you is simply believing. Mark 16:15-18 talks about the signs that will follow those who **believe**.

> *And He said to them, "Go into all the world and preach the gospel to all creation. He who has **believed** and has been baptized shall be saved; but he who has disbelieved shall be condemned. These signs will accompany those who have **believed**: in My name they will cast out demons, they will speak with new tongues; they will pick up serpents, and if they drink any deadly poison, it will not hurt them; they will lay hands on the sick, and they will recover."*

(emphasis added)

We can see that one of the evidences and results of believing is "they will lay hands on the sick, and they will recover."

In Mark 9:23, Jesus Himself said:

> *All things are possible to him who **believes**.*

(emphasis added)

The requirement for releasing healing is not a gift, but rather, a heart that believes.

So what is it that we believe? It is amazing how many people are still unsure of what they are "allowed" to believe

43

when it comes to the supernatural. The political spirit has successfully scared Christians into thinking they can only believe what they can argue and intellectually explain. But, the fact is, you will never fully understand God. Not even one of the aspects of God, such as healing, will ever be fully understood during our time here on earth. Why? Because healing is not what God simply does, but who He is. His very nature is to heal. We will only ever be able to intellectually comprehend so much of His character. That is why Paul says:

> To know the love of Christ which surpasses knowledge.
>
> Ephesians 3:19

Our hearts will always understand far more than our minds will comprehend.

So back to the question, what is it we believe? It is pretty simple really: we believe that what Jesus said would happen, as a result of the cross, actually happened! We believe that through His death and resurrection we have salvation. And the full meaning of salvation is "to be saved, healed and delivered; to be made whole!"

It is an amazing thing to meditate on the results of the cross that we are living in right now! When you come to comprehend in your heart, and not just your mind, that the Spirit of the Living God resides within you, healing is not only simple, but inevitable! In fact, all the gifts of the Spirit are quite simple when you understand that His very Spirit is in you, on you, and all around you. We are grafted into the Vine, and the source of that Vine is flowing to us and through us.

We would do ourselves a huge favour to dwell on God's limitlessness rather than our limitedness. As we begin to think in this way and meditate on this reality, we begin to understand that as we touch someone afflicted, it is the same as heaven touching that person—life flows from us to them. Why? Because Life Himself is within us: Jesus, the way, the truth and *the life*.

As we begin to truly understand that we carry the presence of God Himself, it makes sense that when the Healer shows up, healing happens. We have been telling people that God is love, and God is life. And yet, in the same breath we say, "God gave you that sickness because you needed it . . . He just loves you that much." Then we wonder why the world thinks we are a confusing bunch of depressing religious people!

When Life Himself walks into the room, He does not bring decay; He brings life! Life always produces life. The only thing that Life destroys is death.

We need to truly comprehend the effects of this truth: He is in us and on us. When we are present in any situation, so is He.

So, who is He? He is the Deliverer, the Healer, Love, Life, the Saviour, the Provider, the Truth, the Word, the Creator, the Great I AM—just a few of His names representing His nature. When the Deliverer is present, deliverance happens. When the Healer is present, healing happens. When Love Himself is present, love happens. That is who lives in you and that is who is present with you! Jesus made His *home* in you—not a beach house that He visits once a year. Rather, you are His permanent place of residence.

We were not commanded by Jesus to preach about a Kingdom that we would be heading to one day in the future. He did not commission us to let everyone know that they could go to heaven someday if they believed in

Him. But unfortunately, this has been the gospel message for so long: "Get saved so you can go to heaven one day."

Jesus commanded us to preach a Kingdom that is **presently** at hand.[2] This is a Kingdom that is within us![3] He sent us out to demonstrate this reality. He has not only made a way for us to dwell eternally with Him, but He also made a way to dwell with us! Immanuel!

For those of you who are in paid work, consider yourselves also in paid ministry! Through your work you have been strategically placed by the Lord for this particular time in history! You do not need to go overseas to release the Kingdom; you can do it right where you are! So often we think we need to head off somewhere else, which can be great! But did you know that God is looking for someone in your workplace? That is why you are there! Wherever you are presently positioned, consider yourself "sent." You have been sent by the Most High as an ambassador of His world to your workplace, school, university, home, factory, or farm. Your boss might think he/she pays you, but it is the Lord, in fact, who placed you there intentionally.

I have a friend here in New Zealand who is in the police force and God told him to start loving the ones he was locking up. So he did! He is now seeing the Kingdom of God released to the worst of criminals. These are the ones the world wants to get rid of, but the Lord is snatching them up as His own. We think it is strange but God makes it pretty clear that He desires the "least", the "worst", the "forgotten", the "hated". . . . In biblical terms, these are the "prostitutes" and "tax collectors". Through my policeman friend, the Lord is taking the enemy's best attempts at destruction and transforming them into shining lights for His kingdom. I could fill the pages of this book with testimonies from what he is seeing! This is all because he chose to accept the call to release the

Kingdom in his daily life, even amongst the criminals preparing to be incarcerated. He has seen hardened gang members weeping—not from sadness—but because of God's love. It's amazing that in this earthly prison, he has seen so many people completely set free!

I encourage you to spend time meditating on the reality of the powerful Kingdom within you! Let that reality come alive to you in a fresh way. When it comes to releasing His kingdom, there is nothing more you have to do. He has already qualified you and placed it within you. You are locked and loaded with the Kingdom of God. All that you need to do is pull the trigger! So I encourage you: take a risk daily, take aim and pull the trigger. You will soon discover that this is the purpose for which you were created!

End Notes

1. See Matt. 10:7-8.
2. V. 7.
3. Luke 17:21.

ACTIVATION

1. Take 5 to 10 minutes and meditate on the limitless supply of God's love and power that is flowing to you and through you. Take a moment to become aware of His nearness and presence in you and all around you. When you feel yourself in that place of awareness, begin to take yourself through the following steps:

A. Allow yourself to see the Almighty in His awesome power and glory.

B. Begin to realise that the One you are looking at—the all-powerful, all-glorious One—is the One who is alive and living inside of you.

C. Allow yourself to feel His Spirit dwelling in you. Feel what it is to have Life Himself in you, on you, and all around you.

D. See His limitless power flowing through you to every area of your life: to your family, your friends, to those around you in need. Begin to see what it will look like to see every single need met and every situation transformed by God's goodness.

2. Spend time meditating on the following Scriptures:

A. "For I, the LORD, am your healer" (Ex. 15:26).

B. "He is . . . not wanting anyone to perish" (2 Pet. 3:9, NIV).

C. "Many followed Him, and He healed them all" (Matt. 12:15).

D. "All the people were trying to touch Him, for power was coming from Him and healing them all" (Lk. 6:19).

E. "Large crowds came to Him, bringing with them those who were lame, crippled, blind, mute, and many others, and they laid them down at His feet; and He healed them. So the crowd marvelled as they saw the mute speaking, the crippled restored, and the lame walking, and the blind seeing; and they glorified the God of Israel" (Matt. 15:30-31).

F. "The tongue of the wise brings healing" (Prov. 12:18).

If you have a testimony that comes as a result of reading *The Art Of Healing* or completing one of the activations in this book, I would personally love to hear from you! Email your testimony to:

josh@inflameworshipschool.com

Put the word "Testimony" in the subject line. I look forward to hearing from you.

—Josh

Our grave has been filled
We now dance upon
What was once a hole
Now victory's song
Once locked
In Death's prison
Now free in His kingdom
A dance we've been given
So we will dance on

"Dance On"
by Josh Klinkenberg

3

Another Fun

Night

It was an electric night, full of activity as we gathered in a small room to pray with youth leaders from all over the city. The room was too full for comfort. We were there to minister at a combined youth gathering where hundreds of youth were excitedly pouring into the venue. I knew many of them had come simply to show off to the opposite sex and to have a night out with friends. It was always such a challenge for me to speak to youth. I found it hard to draw them away from their social networks and group texting on their mobile phones. That is, until I discovered the power of God!

Youth are wild when they are introduced to genuine Kingdom lifestyle. They are the most creative generation to walk the planet. Young people just seem to think of things that have never been thought of before. They feel no restriction in their creativity. Because they have not had the years of religious routine that many of us have, they tend to naturally explore the limits "outside the box."

Some of our friends here in New Zealand are seeing the craziest miracles we have ever heard of, and nine times out of ten, it has been through young people! In their innocence, they put no limits to the power of God and so with an adventurous spirit, they launch off and do something that has never been done before! It has become a real joy of mine to raise up passionate young people in such a way where they live the truth of Jesus when He said:

All things are possible to him who believes.

Mark 9:23

As I got up to speak, I soon found that this night was no different than any other—only a few were interested in listening. The rest were wondering who this skinny white fella on stage was interrupting their latest Facebook status update. It is moments like this that I call to mind the testimonies of Jesus we have seen and heard.

I decided to share some of these stories—real life situations touched by the power of God. As I did, I could feel the room begin to shift as these young people began to realise that this Kingdom within them is to be released in their schools, homes, work places, and streets. It was never meant to be limited to a church service on Sunday morning. The real adventure is breaking people out of the enemy's captivity while explosively assaulting the kingdom of darkness and reclaiming the territory held under its oppressive regime here on earth. I had their full attention.

One by one, these youth were taken into an awareness

of the awesome life of creative power that we are born to live in! From that place of their growing interest, there was only one thing to do: display this power we had just been promoting. This is my favourite part! For so long, I had heard the stories, and read about the things that happened long ago in history. But I never truly thought I would ever get to see those same acts of God that we had only heard of in stories from Africa, or the revivalist period from the early 1900s and 1950s. I know there are still so many like me who know these things can happen but feel like we never get to see them firsthand. We only get to hear of miracles in stories that took place in some distant country. Yet to see them for ourselves always seems just out of reach . . . like chasing the end of a rainbow.

So, it was a revelation to me that it is not us who are waiting on God to perform the miraculous; it is God who is waiting on us! I realise now, that I was waiting for something that I already had. I was waiting for some feeling or "filling" that would come overwhelm me and pull the puppet strings in some sort of divine possession, where I am the puppet and God is the puppeteer. But we see throughout Scripture that God is not looking for puppets. He is not one bit interested in "pulling the strings" of control. For that would only result in a lifeless, robotic dance with no true love or friendship shared. And we know that God is really looking for intimate friends to share in a life lived with Him.

I enjoy watching movies, especially ones where the rightful king is restored to his place of rule, and his kingdom, which had been overthrown by evil, is brought back into order and peace is restored once again. There is nothing more frustrating than watching a kingdom fall to wickedness, while the decay of evil spreads, simply because the king is made mute by his own feeling of inadequacy. There are plenty of films where the storyline vividly portrays this very thing. A young king comes into power but very soon is silenced by the fear that he is unworthy and feels inadequate to the task of ruling, when all he really needs to do is open his mouth! Such a Hollywood storyline makes for a good film; but sadly, it is also an accurate portrayal of many believers today. The only difference between the cowardly kings who are incapacitated by fear, and the courageous kings who change nations, is that one is looking for something he thinks he does not have and the other simply realises he has already got it!

Many believers, like me, find themselves waiting for something they think they do not possess; whereas, in reality, our position in Christ has already provided everything we need in order to live out the life God has given us to live! There is absolutely no lack in Christ. He did not leave anything undealt with on the cross. His death and resurrection provided everything that was needed to end the separation and for us to become citizens of His kingdom!

As I said, I realised I was looking for something that I already possessed. I now know that the power of God is not dependent on some "feeling" that comes and goes. It is only dependent on the adoption that we have been brought into. His power is in us and on us because we are His sons and daughters, not because of some feeling we have or do not have. Our sonship is a position in Him that is not altered with the temperament of the day nor does it change with circumstances, and it definitely is not affected by our fragile emotional ups and downs.

I love it when I feel the power of God flow through me and around me! But, the feeling I get when the power of God is flowing is not what causes His power to flow. It happens because His power is already flowing! It is backwards, really, to expect to "feel" something that is not present in order to make it present. The power of God is activated through faith, not our emotional feelings. Thank God for that!

I recall so many times where I was just so tired, or in a "busy" frame of mind, and *feeling* that I was just not in a place that seemed spiritual enough to have God move. And yet, people were healed, and set free in those very moments in such powerful ways! Some of the most significant miracles I have seen by my own hands have been when I least felt like anything was going to happen. And yet, because of sonship, I knew that just because I did not feel anything in that moment did not mean I was any less powerful in Christ.

Again, our adoption is not based on our moods; it is based on what Christ has already done. Still, so many of us live in response to our emotional state and how we feel in the moment which causes real limitations towards what God wants to do through us. This kind of mindset believes that we still need something else rather than responding in faith to what God has already done. All of life is a response; the question is, "What are you responding to?" Are you responding to your own feelings, fears and doubts, or to His Word and what He has said to be true? He has made us His own sons and daughters through Jesus' blood. Take time and allow this to sink in to the deepest part of your being.

So, before me these youth stood. We asked them to gather around those who had needs. I could see they were nervous as they looked for someone who had pain or sickness of some form in their bodies. Very quickly we taught them how to heal the sick in the name of Jesus, and then we set them on course to simply do it! After a few short minutes there was a line of people healed of back pain, shoulder aches, and other annoying ailments.

Another round of prayer resulted in a second wave of victory over the works of the enemy. More backs, necks, and knees were healed! There was rising excitement now throughout the room as these young people realised the power of God was being released through them.

As I was going through the line of those who had just been healed, I came to a young man who held out an arm brace. He told us that he was meant to wear the brace for another five months after which he would have reconstructive surgery. He had broken his collarbone and fractured ribs after being spear-tackled[1] in a rugby game. Because of the break, he had lost some weight due to the fact that the muscles in that arm and shoulder had been inactive. He also had numbness up that side of his neck. But, He was completely healed that night! To prove it, he was swinging his arm around and did twenty press ups, just because he could! It was awesome to see the excitement in the eyes of a young man who just realised the explosive power that is at his fingertips. He later got in touch to let us know that he had returned to his original weight that night as all the muscle had instantly grown back to its original mass! Not only did God heal a completely broken bone, but He also regrew the muscles back to their original size.

One thing we talked to the youth about that night was the power of testimony, and how when you speak about what Jesus has done, it releases the power for that very thing to happen again. Scripture puts it like this:

> *For the testimony of Jesus is the spirit of prophecy.*
>
> Revelation 19:10

If you want to see the miraculous increase in your life, the best place to start is by simply talking about what Jesus has done. When I first discovered this truth I had no stories of my own to share so I just grabbed every audio recording or YouTube video I could about miracles that had happened. I watched A. A. Allen videos, read of Smith Wigglesworth, William Branham, Oral Roberts, Azusa Street, and any other historic accounts of God's raw power in operation. I also listened to those who were seeing breakthrough in this area of the supernatural. Whether their theology was 100% right did not matter. All I wanted to hear was the stories of what God could do through people. By doing this I began to soak myself in the testimony of Jesus! When I spoke at places, I would tell stories of what I had heard others seeing, and I would retell stories from history. And, you know what? It was not long before I had my own stories of what Jesus had done! The testimonies we share in meetings now have turned from the miracles God did years ago in some far off country to miracles that happened just last week by our own hands!

The young man from the youth meeting went and shared his testimony of how God healed him with his good friend who was also unable to play rugby. He had developed gangrene in his left leg and it left him with no calf muscle in that leg. The young man whose collarbone had been healed told his friend how Jesus had grown his muscles back, and then he prayed for the same thing to happen to him. Amazingly, this young player's calf muscle grew back and he was completely cured of gangrene!

This same young man is now back playing rugby with no problems! That is the power of testimony.

The Journey Begins

We have numerous stories like this where Jesus has healed people in phenomenal ways from incurable problems, many without us even praying for them! It is important to note, however, that it has not always been like this for us. My journey of faith is best summed up as a journey of possessing the Promised Land.

It all started several years ago when I was in my early twenties. I was listening to testimonies of miracles and soaking myself in the acts of Jesus which always stirs a hunger deep inside for more. You cannot keep reading about what Jesus has done and stay the same! Thanks to my Dad, I had grown up with an understanding that healing was normal. But even though I had no problem with believing that God heals, I still was not seeing it happen in my own life.

I was newly married and we had just shifted to a small town in New Zealand called Te Aroha. We were given speaking opportunities at our little church where we really started going after healing.

I realised that if I wanted to see people healed, I was going to have to actually pray for people at some point, which, believe it or not, was a bit of a revelation to me. I remember when we first moved to Te Aroha, I would pray everyday, "God, use me to heal the sick. Use me to set people free!" I would pray prayers like that every day.

During one of these prayer times the Lord stopped me and said, "Josh!"

"Yes, Lord?" I replied.

"You want to see people healed, right?"

"Yes, Lord!" I said again, excitedly expecting some

profound life-changing words from heaven that would shape my future forever! The anticipation within me was growing. What He said next, however, was not nearly as profound as what I expected, but it was the very thing that changed my life forever!

"Don't you think it would be a good idea, then, to actually pray for the sick?"

I had to laugh at how simple that was, not even realising that this was indeed the profound, life-changing directive I had been seeking! For months, every day, in fact, I had been praying that God would give me the gift of healing! And in that moment, the Lord showed me that He had given me that gift the very first time I asked for it all those months earlier. I just did not know it because I had not put the gift to use. In order to activate the gift God had already given me, I needed to put myself in a situation where supernatural healing was needed.

I was chatting to the Lord years after this asking Him about the main keys in our life that allow us to see miracles. I wanted to know what it was that we were doing differently that allowed us to see the miracles that we were now seeing. He told me three keys that had become a normal part of our life and I will share more about these later. But the crazy thing was, He said the most significant key that allows us to see the miraculous is that we pray for people. That's it! We must pray for the sick. We pray for situations to change. The supernatural has become our first port-of-call for anything we come across. Could it be that most people do not see others healed simply because they do not pray for them?

James speaks about this:

You do not have because you do not ask.

4:2

THE ART OF HEALING

One of the Father's greatest joys is to give His kids what they ask for. Like I said, He is not interested in having puppets; He desires that we would make bold requests of Him out of an understanding that we are His children, knowing that it is His pleasure to give His children the Kingdom! He loves nothing more than to work with His children to accomplish His plans here on earth.

He is waiting for those of us who will ask Him for the nations, so He can give them to us. He is waiting for those who will ask for the greater works so He can hold our hand and share in the craziest adventures to ever happen on earth in partnership with us!

> *Ask, and it will be given to you; seek, and you will find; knock, and it will be opened to you. For everyone who asks receives, and he who seeks finds, and to him who knocks it will be opened.*
>
> *If you then, being evil, know how to give good gifts to your children, how much more will your Father who is in heaven give what is good to those who ask Him!*
>
> Matthew 7:7-8, 11

End Note

1. "Spear-tackled" means to be driven into the ground head first.

ACTIVATION

For this activation you are going to dream. Dreaming with God allows you to discover the desires of your heart that He has put within you.

In your wildest dreams, what is it you would love to see? It might be that you would love to see people healed and set free as your shadow hits them while you're walking down the street. It might be that you really want to see your home so saturated with His presence, that when people walk into it, they are made completely whole.

What is it you would love to see?

We can have a number of different dreams—all relating to different areas of our life with the Lord. For the sake of this assignment, take one dream and allow yourself to drift away into that dream.

Ask yourself these questions whilst spending some time dreaming with God about that very thing.

- What is it going to feel like?

- What will the atmosphere be like in that moment?

- What will it sound like?

- How will the Holy Spirit be moving in that moment?

Allowing ourselves to drift away in these God-dreams builds faith and expectancy within us. Seeing our dreams in this way can help to create language for the very thing we are asking for. It enables us to pray with specificity and faith because we can "see" what we are asking for.

With love in Your eyes
And power in Your hands
You rescued Your bride
To freedom again
Power and life
Now given to us
God our Redeemer
Our gloriousness

"Hymn of Redemption"
by Josh Klinkenberg

4

The Prayer of

Healing

During my own journey I have discovered that an important part of learning how to possess the Promised Land of healing is learning how to pray. By the time I was married, I had been exposed to the possibilities of the power of God working to see heaven on earth. Yet I was not seeing any of it happen in my own life simply because I had not positioned myself with opportunities to draw on the promises given to me. I was getting hungrier for Him, and the manifestation of His power through me with every passing day. I was like a ticking time bomb ready to go off! All I needed was an assignment.

I had always suffered with bad hay fever as a kid and it was not getting any better with age. I remember waking up one morning and a reality struck me: Hay fever is not in heaven so it should not be allowed here on earth! I was excited because I now had a target in sight. I also realised that the only reason I had hay fever was because I let it stay. This was another simple truth which changed my life!

With authority comes responsibility. We have been given authority here on earth, and with that authority, we need to take responsibility for what has been permitted to take root here on earth. For so long my personal prayer for healing, or help of any kind, was me pointing my finger towards God and saying, "Do something about this!" But soon I realised He was pointing His finger right back at me saying, "I have!"

What I noticed in my own prayer life, and I see the same time and time again in so many other believers, is that the faith-filled prayer that we are meant to release had given way to a form of prayer that is more like begging. We so easily resort to pleading with God, begging Him to move, and doing all we can to try and convince Him to be good. Selah.

We put together our best-sounding case using Scriptures and emotional pleas attempting to pull at the heartstrings of God—as if we need to. We even throw in some bonuses to try and make the deal more attractive to Him! We find ourselves saying things like, "If You do this, God, so many people will see and get saved. . . ." I used to often try to sell these amazing deals to God! Problem is, He won't buy something He has already paid for.

I would often resort to this kind of begging prayer and I have since realised a powerful truth that has changed the way I now pray and it has also changed my relationship with God. This truth has taken me from a place of pointing the finger at Him to taking His hand and enforcing the victory with Him! To beg God for something we need is to neglect the finished work of the cross. To beg God is to call Him a liar, not believing that He is indeed, Immanuel, God with us!

Begging treats Him like some great, distant ruler who needs to be coerced into coming. To beg God for our requests is to neglect the overwhelming love that He clearly has for us, thinking that we need to offer Him a trade off to get Him to show up because deep down we really think, *He does not want to. He only does so when He can get something for Himself . . .* Sadly, so many of us pray as if we believe this. Perhaps we don't say it in words, but we demonstrate what we believe about God by our actions and our prayers. The message that this type of begging prayer sends is that we believe we are more merciful than God. Approaching God with our requests in such a way reveals a clear absence of faith and trust. God is love itself; therefore, we never need to twist His arm into coming to be with us. He is not interested in who can offer Him the best deal. In fact, He is not interested in what He can get at all, for "love does not seek its own."[1] He is interested in us being His beloved. His number one priority for us is to "be-loved." It is who He has made us to be His beloved!

The kind of begging prayer that I used to pray would often sound something like this, "God, if it is Your will, would You please heal this person?" But I came to realise that God does not bless or respond to this kind of prayer. Why? Because He never blesses unbelief. This kind of prayer communicates the fact that we do not really believe Him to be who He says He is. He blesses faith. Unbelief actually repels God, but faith touches His heart. To ask God to do something that He already did on the cross is a request founded in unbelief. To pray, "*If* it is Your will . . ." is to pray from a place of doubt.

James is reasonably straight on this whole subject and he puts it like this:

> *He must ask in faith without any doubting, for the one who doubts is like the surf of the sea, driven and tossed by the wind. For that man ought not to expect that he will receive anything from the Lord, being a double-minded man, unstable in all his ways.*
>
> 1:6-8

We see this principle in action in the story of the Syrophoenician woman.

> *And a Canaanite woman from that region came out and began to cry out, saying, "Have mercy on me, Lord, Son of David; my daughter is cruelly demon-possessed." But He did not answer her a word.*
>
> Matthew 15:22-23

The woman was in the perfect place to see her prayers answered—at Jesus feet—yet He did not even answer her a single word! Why? Because she was trying to get Him to respond to the works of the devil. He will never move in response to the devil. That would give the devil control of God. In Scripture, we only ever see Jesus moved by two things: one is compassion, and the other is faith! The Syrophoenician woman was pleading with Jesus to respond to the work of a demon. But her best pleading brought no response from Jesus.

Then the spiritual atmosphere changes and I believe the woman caught Jesus off guard with her response to His silence.

*But she came and began to bow down before
Him, saying, "Lord, help me!"*

v. 25

The Greek word here for "bow" is *proskuneo*. This
same word is also the word used for "worship." This
determined mother was not about to give in to offence
and let this opportunity pass her by. In this moment she
realised that Jesus was not moved by what the devil was
doing, so she changed her tactics and began to worship
Him!

*It is not good to take the children's bread and
throw it to the dogs. But she said, "Yes, Lord;
but even the dogs feed on the crumbs which fall
from their masters' table."*

vs. 26-27

Jesus gave the woman what seemed like a rude
answer but her response amazed Him. Changing her
position from pleading for a response to the works of the
devil to a position of faith was a transition made through
worship. This mother went from pleading, "My daughter
has a demon! My daughter has a demon!" to a posture of
worship where she knelt before Jesus and poured herself
out on Him. It was a simple cry of faith, "Jesus, help me."
We know it was faith that moved Jesus because of His
response to her:

O woman, your faith is great.

v. 28

Considering how Jesus would have said this in
modern terms, it would be more accurately, "Wow! Lady,
your faith has blown Me away!" He was genuinely amazed.
It was not often that such great faith was demonstrated.
This woman's transition from fear-based pleading to

faith-based prayer became the example and pattern Jesus used to teach His disciples. This kind of faith-filled prayer is what pleases the Father.

I believe that as the woman worshipped, she moved from an awareness of what the devil was doing to an awareness of the supremacy of Jesus. Love moved her from fear to faith.

Jesus responds to faith. There is not much use wasting time trying to cause Him to respond to other forms of petition.

The Lord taught me this when I was dealing with consistent bouts of hay fever. Instead of begging Him for healing, I learned to stand in the authority I have been given in Him and rebuke the hay fever. Jesus did not give us full authority on earth so that we could just ask Him to do whatever was needed. No, He gave us full authority so that as friends and partners with Him in intimate relationship, we would extend His kingdom across the whole earth! He delights in this relationship.

We all learned in Sunday school that Jesus lives within us. Unfortunately most of us regard this as a nice metaphoric thought. It is not; it is truth! Most Christians would agree that if Jesus stood before any problem, no matter how big, and commanded it to "Go!", the problem would vanish instantly. What we need to become more aware of is this: because He lives in us, that same authoritative power is released into whatever problem we face. When we speak, it is the same as if Jesus was speaking. When we touch someone, it is the same as if Jesus were touching that person. Why? Because, it is Jesus touching that person or speaking to that situation through us.

We have to get this: He lives in us. Jesus is the Head

and we are His body in the earth. We are, quite literally, the hands and feet of Jesus to everyone we meet! He gave us the stories in Scripture to demonstrate to us what it was going to be like for us when He took up residence within us. When we speak, we speak in His name. It is not about tagging "in Jesus' name" on the end of a prayer. When He commissioned us as ambassadors of His kingdom, we became the King's spokesperson so that what we say is what He has said. We are marked with His authority in whatever we say and do in His name.

Saltwater or Freshwater?

One of the main reasons so many people do not see the power of God on their spoken words is because they have both saltwater and freshwater flowing from their mouth.[2] What do I mean by that? At times, we can speak carelessly and joke foolishly. Then we pray a prayer and tag "in Jesus' name" on the end thinking that it makes it all legitimate. But, in God's mercy, He withholds His authority from resting on such people so they do not destroy the world around them. Our words create worlds, and they can also destroy them. God is looking for trustworthy stewards of the power that He puts upon our spoken words. In fact, He is looking for people who will not be destroyed by the fullness of His blessing.

Proverbs says:

Death and life are in the power of the tongue . . .

18:21

Once God puts the sobering reality of that on you, it is not something you can just turn on and off. It is important that we recognise that our words carry weighty significance in the Kingdom, as we see evidenced throughout Scripture.

Jesus Himself puts it like this:

I tell you that every careless word that people speak, they shall give an accounting for it in the day of judgement. For by your words you will be justified, and by your words you will be condemned.

Matthew 12:36-37

The Greek word "careless" used in this passage can also be translated "useless." In other words, we will give an account for every useless word we speak. Why? Because our words are meant to create. God intended that the words we speak would hold the power of life and death—life for the Kingdom on earth, death for the enemy.

God is the Creator of all things and we were created in the Father's image and likeness. When God speaks, worlds are created, shaped and formed. So too, when we, His children speak, something powerfully creative is released.

The prerequisite for carrying this kind of powerful authority, however, is to capture the heart of God. Jesus made this profound statement to His disciples:

No longer do I call you slaves, for the slave does not know what his master is doing; but I have called you friends, for all things that I have heard from my Father I have made known to you.

John 15:15

The implication is that once we were slaves, kept in the dark and clueless about the heart of God, but now we are His friends! Through Jesus we have been brought into the light of what the Father is doing. Carrying God's heart into every situation is simply a result of friendship and is not based on us choosing Him, but Him choosing us!

Jesus goes on to say why He chose us:

> *You did not choose Me but I chose you, and appointed you that you would go and bear fruit, and that your fruit would remain.*
>
> v. 16

He chose you and wants you to enjoy the awesome privilege of experiencing the fruit of the Kingdom growing in you and all around you. Jesus continues on to make another mind-blowing statement when He says:

> *Whatever you ask of the Father in My name He may give to you.*
>
> v. 16b

Let's "zoom out" for just a moment and look at the surrounding context of this phenomenal promise. In verse 12 we see Jesus start a new point with a command to "love one another." Then in verse 17 we see Him close this thought by repeating this command. So we can see it is in the context of loving one another that we find this promise of receiving anything we ask for.

I believe it is incredibly significant that this particular promise is framed inside the commandment to "love one another."[3] Jesus put one of the most amazing—not to mention bizarre—promises made to us inside of a "love sandwich." Why? Jesus was showing us that the unlimited life with God is wrapped up in possessing His heart for people.

Asking in His name is, again, not about tagging "in

Jesus' name" on the end of a prayer, but rather, it is making a request of God from a position of friendship found only as we love one another. You simply cannot love Jesus and hate His friends. Loving one another fulfills the requirement Jesus has set for having every request granted from the Father. Becoming a friend of God causes us to think like Him, love like Him, speak like Him, and live like Him. In that place of knowing His heart, we enter into a depth of relationship that allows us to ask anything of the Father. He gives whatever we ask because we are asking not as slaves who do not really know Him, but as friends who share an intimate understanding of His heart.

I love how Paul puts it:

> *All who are being led by the Spirit of God, these are the sons of God.*
>
> Romans 8:14

The Greek word "led" used here also means "to be carried." In other words, those who are carried by the Spirit of God are the sons of God. To be carried by God's Spirit is to see what He sees, love what He loves, laugh as He laughs, and weep as He weeps. It is more than just a directional leading; it is an emotional and spiritual union with the Spirit where we become like Him.

One of the most challenging things to learn here on earth is to love as God loves. When you capture His heart for people, and see them as He sees them, it ruins you. This love makes you whole and breaks you into pieces all at the same time. It heals you and hurts you all at once.

I remember the first time I experienced His love for people. I could not bear to go to places where there was suffering and hardship. I could not bear to see children living in poverty and abuse. I could not handle the pain of it. I know now that we have two options in these moments. We can choose to harden ourselves in an effort to dull the pain of seeing the ones whom God loves hurting each other and being used as pawns, all while the enemy laughs at the misery he has brought to them. The other option is to stay broken—openly exposed to the fullness of His love with all the goodness and pain that comes with it. This choice causes us to take action as compassion captivates our hearts and leaves us with no other way to live but in love—with Him and with those He loves. David speaks about this heart condition:

> *The sacrifices of God are a broken spirit; a broken and a contrite heart, O God, You will not despise.*

> Psalm 51:17

It was a revelation to me that this annoying hay fever I was suffering with was only there because I allowed it. I took responsibility for that fact and then moved into action by also taking responsibility to see it gone for good. I knew it had to go—there was just no two ways about it. So, I committed to seeing the hay fever gone. I decided to rebuke it every day as soon as I woke up. I was so filled with zeal for this that I thought it would happen instantly for sure! Well, a year and a half later, I was still rebuking that hay fever every morning! It had not shifted one bit, but neither had I.

One day, as I was going about my day, I suddenly realised that I did not have any hay fever symptoms where normally I would have had it for sure in my work environment. When I returned home, I said to my wife, "I don't think I have hay fever anymore!"

To be sure, I decided to test it out. We had two cats at the time. One was a big, soft boy we named Oscar. He unwillingly became my "lab-rat" that day as I grabbed him off the couch and rubbed my face all over his fur! I waited for the normal symptoms of itchy eyes and runny nose to kick in, but nothing! From that time on, I knew I was healed!

I remember walking past a Christmas tree in the airport later that year. I had never been able to get close to pine trees without setting off a complete mess of snot and tears. I walked up to that 20-foot high tree and took the biggest whiff I could! For the first time I enjoyed the fragrant scent of that beautiful Christmas tree without being robbed by hay fever. I learned so much from that simple miracle in my own body.

A year or so later I was working with my brother-in-law building a deck on a big farmhouse situated just out of town. Green grassy paddocks and the beauty of the New Zealand countryside surrounded us. As we worked away I started getting the characteristic itchy eyes and runny nose of hay fever that I had not experienced in over a year. I immediately spent time praying, but to no avail. During that week, the symptoms got so bad that I had to leave early because I simply could not see. My eyes were so filled with tears that I could not see the nails to hit them with my hammer. While at the same time my nose had turned into a running faucet that would not stop flowing!

At this point, I was so confused. I thought I had been healed! As I got home I sat there, eyes burning and itchy, unable to see and with a nose that shone like Rudolph the Red-Nosed Reindeer. I sat there defeated and said to God, "What's up with this? I thought I was healed."

He replied simply, "You were."

As He spoke this I caught something. I realised that

this was not a question of whether I had been healed or not. This was a robbery attempt by the enemy that was taking place right under my nose. The enemy was trying to steal my healing and in turn, sabotage my faith that had been built in the process.

In that moment, I realised I was at a crossroads. I could simply stand by and watch this robbery of my healing take place. But in considering this, I realised there was so much more than my healing at stake. It was a robbery of my destiny promised to me: to see the lame walk, the sick healed, and the dead raised!

Then there was option two: take action and put this enemy-thief back in his rightful place—under my feet!

I decided to do the latter. I immediately returned to where I had begun: rebuking the hay fever every single day. For seven long days the thief tried everything he could to steal from me, but like a stubborn old mule, I kept at it. In my zeal I continued binding him, rebuking him and telling him where to go. I figured if the enemy was going to try and hang around, I was going to make it as unpleasant for him as possible. Every time we rebuke the enemy, it is like a jab straight to his teeth.

It's worth mentioning that in my zeal I used to go after the enemy. Zeal is good, but it does not always go hand in hand with wisdom. I now operate in a more mature way by rebuking the enemy and then setting my attention on Jesus in worship. An atmosphere of adoration towards Jesus is highly toxic to the enemy. As we lift Jesus up, He rises with healing in His wings.[4] God is good and He honoured my passion, whilst over time He gave me the wisdom I needed to mature.

Back to my hay fever story. It was only one week before I noticed the hay fever symptoms were all gone and

I am happy to say, it has never returned since!

The tricky thing I observed was that the enemy attacked me with hay fever in a very subtle way. Why? He knows that legally he is not allowed there, unless I let him. We were working on a farm, the farmer was mowing grass, and it was spring. All the natural elements suggested that it was just a result of the time and place I was in. I could have so easily accepted such an argument in that moment. And, most likely, I would still have hay fever to this day. But I chose to stand on my healing and not let the devil rob me of it.

We all know that the enemy comes to steal, kill, and destroy, and the one thing he would like nothing more to take from us is the testimony of Jesus in our lives! Since that day there have been times where I have felt hay fever symptoms try to come back on me again. It may start with the slightest itch in my eye, but all I have to do is command it to leave, and I can feel it retreat faster than it came. It is a petty attempt of the enemy to see if I have forgotten the victory I gained in that area. Maintaining a strong stand in every area of healing we have won is vital.

Hebrews 6:12 tells us to be "imitators of those who through faith and patience inherit the promises." Wholeness is a promise given to us in Jesus' resurrection. For "by His stripes we are healed,"[5] and again, He "has come to seek and to save that which was lost."[6] The word translated, "save," is the Greek the word, *sozo*, which means, "to deliver, protect, heal, save, make whole." You see, wholeness is God's promise to us—complete and total. Therefore, we need to be people who, through faith and patience, take hold of, and maintain our inheritance in this promise.

I long to see a body of people walk in the full inheritance of the cross, who because of their immovable faith and unshakable patience, take full possession of the Promised Land.

Hebrews 10:36 addresses this same point.

> *You have need of endurance, so that when you have done the will of God, you may receive what was promised.*

Endurance is what will walk you into your Promised Land. Faith allows you to do the will of God. Enduring faith goes one step further and allows you to receive what was promised. It takes faith to obey, but it takes enduring faith to receive the rewards of that obedience. Why? Because there can be a period of time between the act of obedience and the receiving of the reward. It's during that time period in-between the two that we need, and exercise enduring faith. This verse implies that although some do the will of God, they still do not receive what was promised simply because they lack endurance. These are ones who follow His voice, but because they do not see immediate results or changes, they give up. When I stand before Him one day, I want to be one whom He knows endured to the end to inherit *all* that He purchased for me. I do not want to find out that I could have seen my wildest dreams fulfilled, but because I lacked endurance, I had stopped just a few steps short.

Ephesians 3:10 is another mind-blowing verse that seems, at times, just too big to be true! Nonetheless, God's Word is faultless. It reads:

> *That the manifold wisdom of God might now be made known through the church to the rulers and the authorities in the heavenly places.*

In making this statement, Paul is showing what is meant to be the result of the preaching of the gospel. The word "manifold" here means "multi-coloured." It is God's plan that His multi-faceted, multi-coloured "wisdom" (which also means, "skill") be revealed. How? Through you and me! God wants to show off His fullness, His skill and wisdom through you. That is why we are destined for "greater works" because the wisdom and skill of God is so vast and endless, it will take an eternity to be discovered!

We get the pleasure of being the "revealed wisdom of God" on the earth. And as if that was not enough, we are also promised, "the things revealed belong to us and to our sons forever."[7] We have received the same promise as Joshua and Caleb received from Moses when he swore to them saying:

> *Surely the land on which your foot has trodden will be an inheritance to you and to your children forever.*
>
> Joshua 14:9

Why?

> *Because you have followed the Lord my God fully.*
>
> v. 9b

When we follow the Lord "fully"—believing Him for all that He is and wants to do—we begin to take back territory for Him that will belong to us and to our children forever! We are giving our children their inheritance!

Age-Old Love Story

The reason I tell the story of my healing from hay fever is because this is where our journey begins! It is the story that marks the beginning of an adventure like no other—an adventure that all of us are able to jump into and discover. It is the story of the ages: the story of a lost kingdom being restored to its rightful place; the story of an ancient King reclaiming a people, who in mutiny, thought they did not need Him. It is the ever-unfolding love story of the Bridegroom and His bride—a bride who pushed Him away to chase down a shadow of all that she already had; a bride who listened to a false god that promised her everything she already possessed and in return left her beaten and alone. It is a story of an unworthy bride being accepted by the very One she betrayed, even unto death.

It is the story of this very Lover who bought back all that His unfaithful beloved lost. It cost Him His own life to give life back to His beloved, but He looked at His beaten, shameful bride and counted it a worthy price to pay. A Promised Land that was once ours was purchased back in the name of our Lover and King.

This is the story that we are in at this very moment in time—the story of the repossessing of that which was once lost to the destroyer and thief. Whether it looks like the healing of hay fever, a sore back, cancer, or even raising the dead, we are participating in this age-old love story! The most ruthless enemy came to rob from this Lover the one thing that He loved the most—His bride. So, in an act of passion and selflessness, this Lover restored His bride to her original place and then decided to give her His very own power and authority to bring the darkest of evils—the same evil that once had her bound in chains and locked in a pit called death—to its knees!

We, as His body, are given the most privileged part in this age-old story. We get to be actively involved in seeing His kingdom's rule enforced across the earth, bringing

79

all things into an encounter with His loving-kindness! He has given us everything we need to complete the takeover.

All that is needed now, in this beautiful love story, is those who will believe!

End Notes

1. 1 Cor. 13:5.
2. James 3:11-12.
3. See John 15:12-17.
4. See Mal. 4:2.
5. 1 Peter 2:24.
6. Luke 19:10.
7. See Duet. 29:29.

ASSIGNMENT 1

Act 1: Meditate on Scripture.

Spend some time meditating on the following Scriptures. Allow the reality of these Scriptures to sink in.

> A. "They [meaning you] will lay hands on the sick, and they will recover" (Mark 16:18).

> B. "Heal the sick, raise the dead, cleanse the lepers, cast out demons. Freely you received, freely give" (Matt. 10:8).

> C. "In the way of righteousness is life, and in its pathway there is no death" (Prov. 12:28).

Act 2: Into the Deep End!

For this activation I want you to step out of your comfort zone and release healing to someone who needs it. You can find this person in your church or home group. You could find them at home; you could find them at work, on the street, in the supermarket, at school—anywhere.

Here is how we are going to do it.

> ✤ *Ask the Lord to highlight a person to you in the next 24-hours that is in need of physical healing.*

God can highlight a person to you in many different ways. But, in any case, this person will stand out to you more than usual.

If they have a physical problem that needs healing, you will usually see some sort of manifestation of that, i.e., a limp, a hearing aid, a sling, crutches, a wheelchair, or bandage, etc. This is how I recognise God highlighting somebody to me.

When you see this person, decide within yourself right now that you are going to jump across the "chicken line" before you think yourself out of it.

✤ *Act quickly, and have fun.*

When you have spotted your "target" for releasing God's love, don't stop and think about it too much or you'll run the risk of thinking yourself out of it.

My goal with this activation is to throw you straight into the deep end. It's incredibly uncomfortable, but it is also the most effective way to learn. With this understanding, I want to give you as little instruction as possible. I simply want you to go out with an understanding that you are commissioned to heal the sick.

✤ *Remember, this person God highlights to you might be someone you know or it might be a complete stranger.*

Here is how I would approach someone who God has highlighted to me: If I can see something obviously wrong with them, I would ask, "What happened?" Although it can be awkward asking someone you don't know a personal question like this, I have found that people actually like to talk about what they know is clearly obvious to others (i.e., walking on crutches, a cast, wheelchair, etc.). After they explain their situation or condition, I would then simply ask, "Would you mind if I pray for you?" I don't bother going into any theological explanation about healing or even that I believe in Jesus. I just ask if I can serve them by praying for them. If they ask, "Why?", I simply reply, "I believe Jesus heals and I believe He wants to heal you."

❖ *Remember, the goal here is not to win someone over to "team healing" or even "team Christianity."*

Our ultimate goal as we engage with people is that they would be loved. Although it happens, it is not very common for someone to respond with a "No" when you ask to pray for them.

❖ *Touch the affected area, if permitted.*

If the person is okay with me placing my hand on the affected area, I would do that while praying a quick prayer: "I command [name the sickness] to leave" and then I'd speak "healing, in Jesus' name." This takes about 30-seconds.

❖ *After praying for them I would ask them to try doing something they couldn't do before.*

This is an important step because it is where most people discover they are healed.

Act 3: Review

Once you have completed activation two, come back and ask yourself these questions:

A. Do you think the person felt loved? If so, then mission accomplished!

B. Was there any noticeable difference after you ministered to them? (Be sure to keep a journal of the miracles you have seen.)

C. How did you feel about it? Were you nervous, excited, flustered, or all of these at once?

D. Were there any areas in the engagement with this person that you feel could be improved upon (i.e., approaching the person, asking them if you can pray, laying your hand on them, asking them to test it out, etc.)? Do any of these areas need review or adjustment?

Night tries to hold us
In the grip of its teeth
At the first sign of sun
It runs like a beast
Into the night
The darkness flees
At the mercy of a single ray
Breaking free
Morning after morning
For thousands of years
The new day dawning
Forever declares
The Son is risen
He broke the night's hold
Freeing mankind
From the days of old

.

"Sunrise"
by Josh Klinkenberg

5

Possessing the

Land

The book of Exodus tells us of the extraordinary story of Israel taking possession of the land that was promised to them hundreds of years earlier. In approximately 1900 B.C., God promised Abram ownership of the land, and then He changed His name to Abraham. It was not until sometime around 1400 B.C., however, that Israel crossed the Jordan River, under the courageous leadership of Joshua, to actually take possession of that Promised Land—some 500 years later! When the writer of the book of Hebrews talks about faith and patience, his prime example of this is Abraham.

The parallels of Israel's expedition into the Promised Land show us a number of spiritual keys for walking in the fullness of life given to us in Christ.

THE ART OF HEALING

A year after leaving Egypt, the Lord instructed Moses to send spies into the Land that He was about to give them.[1] Every one of them, with the exception of Joshua and Caleb, returned with a fear-filled, negative report. This caused all of Israel to take their eyes off of the Lord and focus instead on the giants that lived in that land they were meant to possess. In fear, they grumbled against the Lord, resulting in a 40-year detour through the desert wilderness.

Imagine how different the story would have been had the Israelites not grumbled. Again, this highlights the power of our words and our attitude in the midst of a situation we do not understand. In Numbers chapter 14, we are told how Israel grumbled against Moses and Aaron because of the bad report the spies brought back. The word "grumble" means, "to stop, or to stay permanently." Grumbling is the very thing that will stop you from inheriting the promises over your life. It will cause you to stop and stay permanently in the desert. Even though Israel eventually came into the Promised Land, the generation that grumbled died in the wilderness. Grumbling kept Israel out of their Promised Land and delayed the inheritance by an entire generation. Likewise, it is the same for us today.

Grumbling is not rooted in faith and it is certainly not a fruit of the Spirit. It is one of the main things that prevent the believer from the promised life they have access to by faith through Christ. Grumbling is the act of partnering with fear and doubt. It is a fruit of powerlessness. Joshua and Caleb returned having seen exactly the same scenes as the other ten spies, and yet they had a completely different report. Theirs was founded on a faith in God that enabled them to see from heaven's perspective. Because of this they saw what was possible instead of seeing the impossible.

After hearing the negative report by his companions about the big, bad, ugly giants that were in the land, Caleb takes the stage and makes a bold faith declaration in the opposite spirit:

> *We should by all means go up and take possession of it, for we will surely overcome it.*
>
> Numbers 13:30

Both Caleb and Joshua saw the potential and a battle worth winning. Most people moving in such a bold spirit as this would be accused today of just being an optimist, "ignoring reality." But the truth is, faith sees very differently—it sees with heaven's eyes. Faith is not denying that the mountain is in front of us; rather, faith is simply realising that God has given us the authority to move it.

It took Israel between 400–500 years to claim a promise that was theirs from the very beginning. And once they followed Joshua across that Jordan River, it took them a further five to six years of fighting to clear it out! Imagine living battle-ready, wielding a sword and moving from location to location under the intense stress of war for five long years. That is a long time! Isn't it amazing how Israel was gifted this land hundreds of years earlier, yet they still had to take possession of it by force?

In the same way that Israel was promised a land to possess and live in, we too have been promised spiritual territory in Christ to live from. And in the same way that Israel had to take possession of their land, we too have to take possession of the spiritual territory that is rightfully ours. God promised that fruitful land to Israel, which meant it was rightfully theirs to possess. Yet, they still had to walk in, and by force, claim its possession. In the same way, in Christ, we have been promised spiritual territory that we have yet to walk in and claim. It is going to take a people who are willing to take their "land" by force—not with the "force" of the sword, but by the "force" of faith! Those who forcefully possess their land by faith are a people who are set on pursuing all that has been given to us in Christ, and they are not willing to settle for anything less than its complete fullness.

The primary mandate of Israel was not to simply wipe out the enemy. God could have done that in a day and the job would have been over with. The Father's heart, in this story, is not focused at killing the enemy; it is focused at His people of faith fully possessing the land He had given to them. In the same way, the Father is more interested in us possessing the spiritual territory that He has given to us. Wiping out the enemy is an inevitable byproduct of us taking the land that He destined to be our possession— our inheritance.

Exodus 23:29-30 highlights some amazing keys for us. God is telling Israel how they are going to take possession of the land that He promised them centuries earlier. In this passage, He is giving them His strategy for how this divine takeover is going to take place.

> I will not drive them (the Hivites, Canaanites, and Hittites) out before you in a single year, that the land may not become desolate and the beasts of the field become to numerous for you. I will drive them out before you little by little, until you become **fruitful** and **take possession** of the land.
>
> (emphasis added)

In the context of reclaiming and repossessing our spiritual territory, the "beasts of the field" from this Scripture are synonymous with demonic spirits. The

Lord, in His wisdom, does not empty out the land ahead of the Israelites knowing that they are not yet numerous enough to fully possess the Promised Land. His heart is that Israel would be fruitful enough to fully possess the land.

We see this same principle in a story that Jesus tells.

> *Now when the unclean spirit goes out of a man, it passes through waterless places seeking rest, and does not find it. Then it says, "I will return to my house from which I came;" and when it comes, it finds it **unoccupied**, swept, and put in order. Then it goes and takes along with it seven other spirits more wicked than itself, and they go in and live there; and the last state of that man becomes worse than the first. That is the way it will also be with this evil generation.*

Matthew 12:43-45, emphasis added

The unclean spirit is cast out of a person, but He makes it clear that this same spirit is able to return with seven spirits even more wicked than itself. Why? Because the place is unoccupied. When a piece of spiritual territory is left unoccupied, the enemy is only too happy to take up residence there.

The Lord's goal here is not to destroy the enemy—that is the easy part. The goal is that we would take possession of the land. This is the very act of the restoration of all things. It is in taking possession that we see His original order restored. In God's wisdom, He does not rid the land of "enemies." Instead, He leaves them for us to defeat. In so doing, we are exercised in how to fight and utilise the tools He has given us—authority and power. In this way, we are ruling our territory and displacing the enemy who once resided there. Driving out the enemies

91

that inhabited the land we have been given ownership of builds within us the character and fruitfulness needed to possess that very territory. God's ultimate plan for us to take possession of our spiritual Promised Land is to do it little by little—leaving time for us to become fruitful. And, in our fruitfulness, the end-goal of possession is achieved.

God's plan has not changed today. He is the same, yesterday, today, and forever. His strategy for Kingdom takeover here on earth was revealed thousands of years ago! It is little by little—allowing time for fruitfulness, and ultimately, for full possession. The Hebrew word "possession" used in Exodus 23:30 means, "to inherit, or to occupy." His plan is that we would become so fruitful in the spiritual territory He has given to us, that we would completely "occupy" it, leaving no room for the enemy to have any ground.

In this day and age we are forever bombarded with terms that are deemed to be synonyms for success, words like, "acceleration," "rapid growth," and "instant increase." These terms are all feeding today's microwave-culture of "success means now!" Sadly enough, this culture is almost more prevalent in the church than it is in the world.

I love to see passion and zeal for the Lord, and I love a heart that is contending for the fullness of the promises here and now. But, we have to realise that in our passion and zeal—whether we are running or walking—the land is still taken only one step at a time. A nation is changed by simply loving one person at a time. As we advance in this way, we can very quickly look back and see the vast amount of territory that we have not only claimed, but also possess!

Many people have seen supernatural breakthrough in their lives at some point, whether in the area of healing, deliverance, provision, or direction. Almost all believers, these days, have seen the Lord move in their lives in a supernatural way somewhere along the line. However, the most common thing I have witnessed in this area of the supernatural is that many believers hold a passive stance—waiting for God to "intervene" whenever it is convenient for Him to do so. One of the major keys for us in seeing consistent miracles in our lives is the realisation that He is waiting for us to put ourselves in a position that places a demand on His goodness. And going hand-in-hand with this is the understanding that when we are not seeing breakthrough come, it is simply because we have stepped into new territory that we have yet to possess. Having this understanding enables us to continue in faith and to keep pressing forward in the pursuit of the fullness He has given us. When we start seeing repetitive miracles in an area where we once saw none, we understand this to be a sign of becoming fruitful in that particular area, and that "possession" of this "piece of the Promised Land" is well underway!

It took me a year and a half to get a tiny piece of land that was once inhabited by hay fever. But once I had taken possession of that small square footage of spiritual territory, I used it as a "beachhead" to extend the boundaries of the territory I had possession of for the Kingdom. How did I do that? Well, when I saw my own breakthrough in the "land" of hay fever, I made sure I stewarded that victory by putting it into practice whenever I came across someone with hay fever. I wanted to become as fruitful as I could be in that "piece of land." When you receive your miracle, know that it is not meant to stop there. By receiving a miracle, you have just been given an opportunity to take ownership of something for the sake of the Kingdom. Remember, the goal is possession, and that happens through becoming fruitful.

I remember when I first saw fibromyalgia healed. I did not even know what it was, but a lady who had it in her arm was healed of it. Then I was in another meeting and a second lady was healed of it in her arm. My ears pricked up as she shared what Jesus had just done for her. I went away from that meeting knowing that we had taken a step forward into new ground where we were starting to see new enemies defeated. As I continued to advance from my small beachhead in the Spirit, I began to see more and more healings take place, and more and more varied problems being defeated for the Kingdom.

It was less than a year later that I remember we were in a little church here in New Zealand and a lady was set free from eighteen medically recognised points of pain. She had suffered from fibromyalgia that riddled her body with continuous pain for a significant amount of time. The pain was so severe that she was unable to even lift her arms above her shoulders—that was, until Jesus healed her. Afterwards, she was waving her arms in the air, announcing, "All the pain is gone!" with tears streaming down her face. It blew me away to see the ground we had taken. We just had our heads down, doing what we were commissioned to do, and the next thing, we look up and found we were on the verge of taking possession of a piece of land that was once owned by fibromyalgia!

It was not long after this incident that I shared this particular testimony in another small church here in New Zealand. After the meeting a woman came up to me and said, "I have the same thing."

I kind of looked at her blankly, and she continued, "I have eighteen points of pain in my body from fibromyalgia."

I was amazed. I have never heard of that many points being medically recognised; and now, out of nowhere it seemed, there were two women with exactly the same thing. God really had my attention and I knew we were now deep into this new territory! This woman went on to explain that her pain was like having six-inch rusted nails pushed into her body.

"Is the pain there now?" I asked.

"Yes," she replied. "The worst two points are in my upper arms." With that, I placed my hand on the woman's shoulder, rebuked the pain, and released healing to her.

"Can you test it out now?" I asked.

The woman grabbed the points in her arms and sympathetically said that it was still there. She had one of those looks on her face that a grandmother offers to her grandkids when they try something, only to miserably fail. Her look to me said, "It was nice of you to take the time to pray, young man." She thanked me and turned to walk away.

That could have been the end of an awkward situation, but I hate the thought of letting sickness laugh at the power of God. I grabbed her by the arms, right where that pain had taken up residence, and said, "Let's just pray again."

Still trying to make me feel better with her sympathetic look, she just stood there as I again rebuked the pain. This time I felt it leave her—I knew something had happened. So I said again, "How is that?"

She was still playing the caring grandmother as she reached for her arms again to satisfy the request of this overly-confident young man.

Just as she started to say, "It is still—", she stopped mid-sentence and her face immediately changed. Looking deep into my eyes she half-spoke, half-whispered in a mystified tone, "It is gone!"

It was such a privilege to see her face as she slowly started to walk away, trying to make sense of what just happened. As she left, she looked like she had just seen a ghost, still prodding at her arms, partially in awe, partially in shock, at what had just happened to her.

In these moments where I see a significant breakthrough take place, I love turning to someone with hay fever and praying for them. It is my twelve memorial stones on this side of the Jordan[2] that remind me of the land that the Lord brought me out of. Selah.

We have a powerful inheritance in the life of Christ. An inheritance is given upon a person's death; but the inheritance itself is a result of that person's life. In the life of Jesus, we find our inheritance. A part of that inheritance is that all who came to Him were healed. And even further than that, anyone who even *touched* Him was healed![3]

We have a Promised Land that was given to us as an inheritance on that cross 2,000 years ago when Jesus died and rose again. He took back the keys of death and hell. He took back the dominion and authority that we lost in the garden and charged us with the task of taking possession of the territory purchased for us. Jesus died so we would have an inheritance. He rose so that we could claim it with power! He charged us with the most awesome of tasks: to see the promises of God made to countless generations before us answered! We get to take back the very dominion that Adam lost in the garden. And the best part is that He gave us His resurrection power to do it! What a blast!

There are people today who have taken such ground in the area of healing that they literally have 100% success rate in seeing healing over specific afflictions. I know of ministries who have twelve or thirteen specific diseases of land they possess, so that as soon as they touch a person with one of those conditions, that person is instantly made well. Heidi Baker, who founded Iris Global ministries in Mozambique, has 100% success rate over deafness. Any village they go to in that country, her and her team *know* that every deaf person they pray for will be healed.

People all over the earth have started to walk in this reality already. The invitation to heal the sick, cast out demons, and raise the dead was not exclusive. In fact, it was all-inclusive! Come and join in the fun!

End Notes

1. Num. 13.
2. See Josh. 4.
3. Luke 6:19.

ASSIGNMENT 2

For this activation, I want to stretch you even further. Here is your assignment for this week.

❖ *Release healing over five or more people outside of a church setting.*

You can find these five people anywhere except at a church gathering. You might find one of these five while you're out shopping, or at your school, your work place, your friend's house, your neighbour, the gym, the beach, at a restaurant or cafe, or even at the gas station. One of my goals is to see a person saved, healed, and delivered while waiting at the traffic lights in my car!

Remember, the goal is that each person would be loved. We are simply using healing to shine His goodness and love towards them. Ultimately we want people to encounter the love of the Father and to share a connection with Him. Until then, our mission is to serve them with His love and goodness.

Tips

1. Remember to have fun. Approach people with love and in a light-hearted manner.

2. Don't think yourself out of it. Step over the chicken line. It is never easy, but it's always worth it.

3. Keep your prayers short and to the point.

4. Exercise your authority and command the sickness to go.

5. Release healing and life in Jesus' name.

Taking captive the cold
This warmth transforms
The night into home
With fire in His eyes
And life in His hands
The earth is freed
From the shadowlands
Nowhere is there a
Hint of a fight
As light consumes
The darkness of night
Victory is in
The hands of the Son
This war was over
Before it begun

"Sunrise"
by Josh Klinkenberg

6

Three Main

Keys

I remember many years ago hearing a prophet retelling his story. As a young man he was incredibly gifted at interpreting dreams. One day an elderly lady came up to him after he had interpreted several dreams for different people. She asked the young prophet, "How do you do that?"

Assuming that she was impressed by him he answered, "I don't know . . . I just do."

To his surprise the woman said in reply, "Oh, that's a real shame. 'Cause now you'll be the only one who knows how to do it."

When I heard this story I said in my heart to the Lord,

"Father, would You teach me how these gifts work? I not only want to move in the gifts of Your Spirit, but I also want to understand how to invite others into the same experience."

It was from that time on that the Father began to show me the keys which enabled us to see the miraculous in us and around us. In this chapter, I want to look at the three main keys that we have come to know. These three keys are incredibly simple, and yet sometimes, incredibly hard to live by. They are not hard because they require some great skill, but because they require surrender. These three keys cost us daily: our pride, with our so-called "reputation"; the sense of entitlement we hold on to when offended; and finally, our need to "look good". It is important to note that the small price we pay in surrender does not compare to what we receive from Him in exchange!

Key 1: Conquer Offence

We have had to climb over, smash our way through, and sometimes drag ourselves under the walls of offence that have tried so incredibly hard to stop us. Offence is exactly that—an "o"-shaped "fence" that will establish the boundaries in which we will live.

An offence caused by another person can be extremely hard to let go of. It can be all too easy, at times, to nurse a grudge for a long while against the one who offended us. This will only serve to rob us of so much—in particular, an intimate relationship with the Lord. The crazy thing is, if you hold onto it long enough, it may even cause you to become dependent on it, making you feel as if you *need* it to live. So, why hold on to something that is costing you everything, but pays nothing in return?

When we become a person who is easily offended, it is often because we have a root of offence towards God, and its outworking is being easily offended at everyone else. But Jesus said:

Blessed is he who does not take offence at Me.

Matthew 11:6

The word "blessed" in this passage also means "happy." Happy is he who is unoffended at God. At times, this can be a lot harder than we think. Why? Because God's ways do not always make sense to us and they can even seem quite offensive at face value.

If you feel like this is you, ask the Lord a simple question, "What is it that I am offended at, Father?" You may already know. I still encourage you to ask Him this question anyway, because at times, there is something much deeper which we are often unaware of. The Holy Spirit will reveal to us what it was that caused offence. Oftentimes when offence has taken root in our heart, it can be traced back to a situation that caused us to believe a lie about God and His character.

If the Father has shown you a situation in your life that has caused offence towards Him, ask, "What lie have I believed about You as a result of this situation?" From there, receive forgiveness for believing a lie, and ask the Holy Spirit to reveal the truth in its place so that we would know who He really is in that aspect of His character.

It's important that we renew our experience with the Father in these areas where offence has taken root. For example, if I found that a situation caused me to feel alone and abandoned, I might find that I believed a lie that the Father was not with me in that time. Once I have identified this lie for what it is, I can turn to Scripture

103

and see the truth that He never leaves us or forsakes us. Although this is good, it is important that truth does not stay intellectual; it has to become experiential. So in this example, in order to fully know this truth, I have to actually experience His nearness and His presentness to cancel out the feeling of absence that led me to believe a lie. A renewed experience with the Father leads to renewed trust and faith.

A good thing to do once you see what it was that caused the offence is to ask Jesus, "Where were You in this situation?" And then, "What were You doing?" Once we see Him for who He really is in that situation, we will experience truth, and the truth will set us free. In essence what we are doing is asking the Father to reveal to us Jesus, who is the Truth. Truth sets us free because every area of bondage in our heart can be traced to a lie. Replacing those lies with truth is the very journey of being transformed by the renewing of our mind.[2]

My wife is one of the hardest people I know to offend. Believe me, I have tried! But when our son was born and was rushed straight to an NICU in critical condition where he stayed for close to three months, she was overwhelmed with offence towards God. It wasn't until several years later that my wife asked Jesus where He was in that moment and what He was doing when she felt so alone. He answered her, and as a result, she was completely set free in a huge way!

The Syrophoenician woman whom we talked about earlier, had the best excuse of anyone in history to be offended. The Son of God Himself—by whom all things were made and have their existence, the One who even designed this lady—called her a dog! In that moment she was at a crossroads and could have taken offence at Jesus' words to her. If she had done that, however, that's all she would have been left with. But what she chose to do instead was crash through that offence hurled at her right into an inheritance, which resulted in her daughter being blessed with complete healing. Furthermore, the ripple effect of that story is still affecting history today—thousands of years later! What an amazing victory she stepped into that day!

I see so many people unable to see God move through them because they are so hung up over what He has not yet done. What they don't realise is that with every step taken, they are getting closer to that very piece of land being re-possessed for Him and His kingdom! Remember, He is faithful to the end and He will finish what He started! He started a Kingdom takeover here on earth and He *will* finish it! Do not let offence, however, rob you of the joy of partnering with Him in this.

As Mordecai once said to Esther when he urged her to step into her destiny:

> *If you don't do this, God will use someone else, and the only ones who will lose out will be you and your family. But why not you? Why not now? How do you know that you were not born for this exact thing?*[1]

It is important to understand that holding onto offence only serves to trap us. We are the only ones who lose out. We know that God will finish what He started; His kingdom will increase and cover the earth as the waters cover the sea. The Kingdom takeover is inevitable and His plans will come to completion! Whether or not we are a part of the journey, that is up to us. It is to His joy that He invites us to participate in this great adventure. Never allow offence to stop you from joining the great enjoyment of partnering with Him to this end. Sacrificing all offences is such a small price to pay for the pleasure of journeying with the Holy Spirit.

I ask you, as Mordecai asked Esther, who is to say that you were not born for this very thing? I actually believe God created you to release heaven on earth, to take ground for His kingdom. And His kingdom is so vast that the earth will be covered with His glory until every part of society, every person, and every single bit of creation is so filled with Him and His presence, that heaven and earth look exactly the same!

Indeed, you were born for such a time as this! So why not you? Why not now?

For those who have been overcome with offence, whether for a month, a year, a decade, or a lifetime, your hope is this: you have a unique opportunity to overcome in that area that will not only free you *from* something, but will also release you *into* something. There is an inheritance waiting for you on the other side of that "o"-shaped fence. For the sake of the Kingdom, take down that fence and take hold of a new life of freedom!

Those of you in this position take a moment and pray this prayer. Remember, God does not blame you for feeling the way you feel. He understands and knows everything you have had to walk through.

Father, I need Your help. I don't want to be trapped by offence anymore. Even if I can't see what has caused it or where it came from, I know You do. Help me to release forgiveness, even where it hurts me. Help me to forgive, even where I have been treated unjustly. Holy Spirit, I want to be free and I don't want offence to rob me of the freedom You have given me any longer. Would You come right now and set me free? Would You take this offence in my heart and turn it into a memorial to the beauty of Your freedom in my life? Teach me how to receive forgiveness and freedom in its fullness. I also pray, Father, that this month You would renew my experience with You in this area. I need to feel Your love and acceptance again and I trust that You want to show me Your love and acceptance again. I give You permission to flood me with love and acceptance this month. I love You, Father. Thank You for continually calling me forward into freedom.

Jesus, An Offence

Romans 9:33 is one of those verses I wish was not in the Bible. But it is also one of those verses that makes a lot of sense when you begin to look at it openly and objectively.

> *Behold, I lay in Zion a stone of stumbling and a rock of offence, and he who believes in Him will not be disappointed.*

The Father Himself puts a stone of stumbling, a rock of offence, right in the centre of our Promised Land. We can see from the second part of the verse that this stone of stumbling is not a thing; it is a person! The most offensive part of it all is that this person looks, sounds, smells and feels just like Jesus. Why? Because it is! He is the stone of stumbling and the rock of offence.

With this in mind, let us look at this Scripture another way:

> *Behold I* [the Father] *lay in Zion* [the Promised Land] *a stone of stumbling and a rock of offence, and he who believes in Him* [Jesus, the stone of stumbling and the rock of offence] *will not be disappointed.*

It is extremely unsettling to run into your King and Lover in the midst of crisis only to find He is the most offensive person you have ever met! Your heart recognises that this is Life Himself, but your mind wants to run away in offence.

Jesus made an astounding statement that brought an immediate response of offense:

> *He who eats My flesh and drinks My blood has eternal life.*
>
> John 6:54

Notice that it was not strangers who were offended and walked away. No, it was many of His disciples who withdrew, and from that day onward chose not to walk with Him anymore. Coming to Jesus is easy. Staying with Him will cost you—specifically, your right to be offended.

But all of this is only for the sake of taking us deeper into a heart-to-heart relationship with the Father. Surprisingly, He is not all that interested in our desire and need to have it all sorted out intellectually. In the end, He is not going to question us theologically. He simply requires this one thing: that we know Him. The kind of relationship He is after is an intimate depth of love shared between the two of you that makes no logical sense at all. It is like a married couple that is truly deeply in love with one another. They may not agree on everything, but their love for each other supersedes human logic and intellectualism so that it does not matter. The heart-to-heart love they share overrides everything else. This is His desire for the relationship He shares with us.

Jesus will often offend us in the centre of a Promised Land that He has given to us to possess because He wants to see if our heart for Him will enable us to step over the stumbling block of offence. Every offence that comes our way is an opportunity to go deeper in love with Him. He wants to see if our love for Him means more to us than our right to be offended.

An offence occurs when a rule or law is broken. As our relationship develops with Him He progressively breaks the laws and rules that we have set up inside of ourselves which only serve to maintain separation. These rules and laws are the very things that set limits on our relationship with Him. When the time comes where He reaches one of these separational boundaries in our heart, He will purposely operate outside of these parameters we have so carefully put into place. In doing so, He gives us an invitation to jump over that boundary line and explore new depths with Him.

Remember, offences are simply "o"-shaped "fences" that we place around our heart as boundaries to maintain separation rather than facilitate intimacy. When an offence is brought to light within us, remember that it is an exciting time of relational development with the Lord Himself!

The best part of the verse from Romans 9 is the last phrase:

> *And he who believes in Him will **not** be disappointed.*
>
> v. 33, emphasis added

That is an amazing promise! Choosing to believe in Him through the offensive hurdles that stand in the way of deeper intimacy enables us to receive the promise so that we "will not be disappointed." When we choose to believe God for who He says He is, the world around us will attempt to test and challenge that choice. But we have His Word, so that as we believe in Him, we will not be disappointed.

I am believing God for the fullness of the life given to us on the cross all those centuries ago. I am believing God that I will possess spiritual territory that I never even knew existed. I am believing God that every person I lay hands on, everyone I speak to, everyone I pray for walks away in wholeness. And the best part of it all is God's promise: I will not be disappointed!

Jesus will work outside of our understanding, which is intellectually offensive. But in doing this, He gives us the opportunity to know Him like never before. Believing in Him will never leave us disappointed.

> Blessed [happy] *is he who does not take offence at Me.*
>
> Luke 7:23

What I have come to see on our own personal journey is that one of the hardest things to do is to choose to believe God in the midst of such deep pain. We naturally try to protect ourselves from pain—both physically and emotionally. So, when a situation emerges that causes extreme emotional pain, the most common and immediate gut reaction is to protect ourselves in any way possible. Although we cannot always prevent pain from hitting us, we can prevent it from ruining us. When we live with such hurt but do not deal with it, we live our lives around the avoidance of further pain. We avoid any situation that could possibly cause more hurt—even in the slightest form. The danger of living in this way for too long is that we end up hardening our heart towards others' situations which then leaves us unable to genuinely demonstrate the compassion of Jesus.

One of the hardest things I personally had to deal with on our journey was this whole area of "believing God." Even the thought of believing God for my son's healing was too scary to confront, so I would just bury it and leave that whole side of my relationship with Him alone. Any time the issue of my son's healing came up I would quickly shut down and try to protect myself by putting a bit of distance between me and the Lord.

When God began to work on this area of our relationship He did so in such a gentle way, knowing the incredible pain of the open wound in my heart. The Lord is never harsh or easily frustrated with those whom He loves. He understands the hurts that often prevent us from drawing near into a deeper relationship. He patiently and lovingly takes the time needed to walk with us, cry with us, laugh with us, hurt right alongside of us, rejoice with us—all the way through into wholeness.

As God began this walk with me, He showed me that one of the greatest fears I was avoiding was the *what-if-it-doesn't-happen?*–fear. When you are able to let Him take this particular fear out of your hands, you will see that which seemed unmovable simply dissolve in His pure and perfect love. It is here that you will find yourself standing in one of the deepest places of trust that you have ever experienced!

I was too afraid to even pray for my son because the fear that nothing would happen was so strong. It was really a fear of feeling rejected by God. In my attempt to protect myself, I could not even pray for my own son. I was paralysed at the thought of further hurt hitting me, because unknowingly, I had believed the lie that I could be rejected by God. Living in this state of such hurt I was unable to even think about the possibility of more hurt coming my way. My solution in this state of hurt was to avoid anything that even slightly resembled faith for healing.

One of the weird things about having a child like

my son is that everyone feels it is their duty to tell you about every person they know who has had something terrible happen to them. For some reason, people seem to think that it will make you feel better to hear about others who are also in the midst of incredible pain. I remember people would often tell us of other children who were facing incredible hardships, and as soon as they started, I would shut off—instantly numbing myself to any emotional involvement in their story. I just could not stand to hear anything that would cause me further hurt. And because I was so afraid of pain, I began to lose all sense of feeling towards anything. I was en route to emotional suicide.

God, being a God of heart-to-heart friendship, is not an easy person to be around when you are in this kind of place. He keeps calling you, pulling you, drawing your heart back to Him. I could only ignore it for so long before it broke me. Trusting God in a place of complete uncertainty is not something that is easily done. It is the scariest thing imaginable to a person in a position of overwhelming hurt. To let the walls of self-protection down and stand transparent and naked before Him is incredibly terrifying. Those who have been in this position will know what I mean. It took my wife and I years to stand before Him again, transparent and unoffended.

It is such a scary thing to give someone access to your heart when it has suffered such pain. To let the Lord near again is one of the greatest fears hurting hearts have to conquer. To keep our hearts open to the Lord when we walk through great pain requires incredible brokenness. And when I say brokenness, I do not mean sadness. There is a big difference between sadness and brokenness. It is this brokenness that will cause you to forgo the right to offence and choose Him instead. It is brokenness that says, "I am not going to shut myself off to love even though it is going to cause me incredible pain." Even today I am brought to tears almost every time I meet, see, or hear of a child suffering in any way. It still causes unbearable heartache. But it is not a heartache triggered by hurt anymore; now my heart aches because of love. I am moved by His love and compassion for those suffering. It is this depth of love that gives me a perspective of the Father's heart for people that few are willing to experience because it costs so much.

> *A broken and contrite heart, O God, You will not despise.*
>
> Psalm 51:17

For those who have come to know such pain, all I can say is that even though it will cost you everything to overcome the offence and hurt, it is every bit worth it. The freedom with God on the other side of that hurt is beyond description. Those who refuse offence and hurt will be the most radical representations of His love on this earth. Step into Your inheritance and begin the journey of trusting God fully as you dismantle all the "o"-shaped "fences" in your heart. This walk of freedom from offence into intimacy is a life so beautiful, with a relationship so valuable, that words are not able to describe it! I have determined no cost is too great for intimate friendship with my Father in heaven.

If you are one who has met with this kind of pain and has since lived in a way where you find it hard to trust the Father with your whole heart, I want you to pray this with me:

> *Father, I love You and I need Your help. You know I want to trust You with my whole heart but I do not know how to get to that place. Would You please help me, Father? I give*

You permission to come and break down the boundaries I have set up in my heart out of fear. Come and remove anything that is limiting our intimacy. I need You to show me how to trust You. Please take my heart right here, right now, and heal it of the hurts that have taken hold. Help me to release forgiveness right now. Help me also to receive forgiveness right now.

Now in your own time, allow the Father to move into every part of your heart. Take a moment and be still, allowing all the parts of your heart that you have kept from Him to be flooded with His presence. Take all the hurt, and all the pain, and give it to Him. He has seen it all along. It does not disgust Him or surprise Him. He will simply take it from you and you will see that it is not yours to hold on to anymore. Take some time to let forgiveness sink into your heart—both for yourself and for others.

Key 2: Stubbornly Believe

Even when every natural thing is telling you otherwise, choosing to believe who God is simply because it is who He said He is, will be extremely powerful in your life. We have countless well-meaning people try to console us by telling us such things as, "God loves your son just the way he is," and, "He made him that way for a reason." For some reason, whenever I preach on healing I get at least one person who feels it is their God-given duty to crush any trace of hope, and in an effort to be the bearer of truth, they kindly remind us that God allows this kind of thing because it is some sort of (twisted) blessing.

We usually smile and just thank the person, knowing that to say anything in response to this untruth would not result in a change of heart on their part—or ours. Often people with such views fit into one of two categories: they either have no idea about what is involved in the lives of those suffering with such incredible hardship (nor do they have any intention of finding out), or they have accepted defeat.

In regards to the first case, as I said in a previous chapter, people would do well to get involved with those who are living with such day-to-day hardships. It would be a welcome wake-up call to many in the body of Christ.

In the case of the latter, I pray for these ones that they would see that they are unknowingly standing in victory's doorway, but oftentimes facing the wrong way. They are, in fact, looking back at the raging storm without realising that all they need to do is turn around to see victory directly in front of them.

Every time I see a child suffering in any way, I am reminded again: keep going, do not give up, pursue God. For their sake, I must see this Promised Land taken! I owe them that much. I do not mean to sound harsh, but it bothers me when I see powerless Christians trying to convince me—or others—to settle in defeat.

> *Even though I walk through the valley of the shadow of death, I will fear no evil, for You are with me.*
>
> Psalm 23:4

Remember, this valley of death is only a shadow. You cannot tell what a person is like by looking at the surface of the ground where their shadow is being cast. And yet, that is often what we do with God. We come up with our own theology of Him which allows for our natural circumstances to be left unchanged instead of realising it is not God who needs to change in order for things to make sense. Rather, it is this natural world that needs to be brought into alignment with His will.

Jesus taught us to pray, "Your kingdom come, Your will be done." He told us to pray for His will to be done because we live in a world where there is plenty going on that is not His will. God's will and His heart is that we would usher in His kingdom upon this earth through intimate relationship with Him. The answer to this prayer is to make earth like heaven. He is looking for "on earth as it is in heaven," not the other way around.

Do not let anything steal away the fact that God is healer. We need to choose to stubbornly believe Him for who He is because the enemy will do all he can to convince us otherwise.

Bill Johnson, Senior Leader of Bethel Church in Redding, California, said something that has become one of my favourite quotes:

> *I will not sacrifice the idea that God is good on the altar of human reasoning in order to find an answer for what I don't understand or can't explain.*

Believing God, for the most part, makes no earthly sense, and the annoying truth is that sometimes He even goes out of His way to ensure that it does not make sense. But standing on who He has said Himself to be is what positions us for the Romans 9:33 promise:

> *He who believes in Him will not be disappointed.*

God's will is to save, to make whole, to set free, to love, to bless, to shine His goodness! To have faith in Him here on earth is an incredible privilege. We are not going to need faith in heaven as we know it here on earth. It is something we only get the chance to experience here.

God is all-loving and outrageously good. Some people seem to need an angry God to justify their anger. In the face of offence and unrelenting opposition, we stubbornly believe God is who He said that He is. It makes no sense at times, but He never promised that it would.

Selah.

Key 3: Position Ourselves

We do not just talk about the supernatural; we anticipate it and create an environment of expectation in our life to receive it. We even put ourselves in places where God's power has to move, otherwise we will look like idiots! I have stood before rooms filled with people who do not even believe that God still does "that stuff" today and declared before them, "God is the healer, and He loves to heal!" Because I can see that the people do not believe my words, the only thing left to do is demonstrate it! Not only do I show them that He heals, but I show them that He heals through them! *They* pray for the sick and the sick get healed. But the point is, in those moments, the temptation is to water down the power of God to make it more "people-friendly" so as to not cause any conflict.

The Promised Land that we have in Jesus includes healing, but is also vastly more than that. My wife and I were financially poor when we had our first son. His full-time care at home took us both out of work. In New Zealand we have an awesome government system that is set up to help people in our situation. The problem we had was that our situation did not fit into any of their boxes and so it took months for them to figure out what to do with us. Then after they finally sorted us out a year later, they told us they had it wrong and we owed them

$20,000! It was a whirlwind time of uncertainty for us. Long story short, the $20,000 finally got wiped off as their mistake and they put us on the right type of financial assistance. While we were thankful for this, it still left us short each week. We were unable to afford rent, power and food, let alone petrol and car maintenance that was needed to get to and from the hospital.

My wife and I made a decision in that time that, no matter what, we would give sacrificially out of our own need. We decided that we were not going to let poverty rob us of generosity. So we gave. The amount of times we went to the cupboards to grab some food only to find it empty was crazy. But without fail, God provided. We decided to trust Him and we can now truly say that we know Him as provider. Every time we were running low and had nothing left, as if on queue, someone would knock on the door with several bags of groceries.

At the time of this writing, our financial position on paper has not changed much at all but, through generosity and intentional giving, we have taken some serious ground in that whole area. We have been given our needs in abundance and we are now receiving our wants. We have been given thousands upon thousands of dollars over the years—always at the perfect time. We make a point not to "advertise" our need to others. We simply choose to trust in His loving kindness.

Do not get me wrong, being in need is not comfortable by any stretch of the imagination. But to know Him as Provider is worth every bit of discomfort we have been through.

The point is this, being in a place of need positions you to take ground. Jesus said that He came to preach the gospel to the poor—to those who have need.[3] He also said:

Blessed are the poor in spirit, for theirs is the Kingdom of heaven.

Matthew 5:3

Being "poor in spirit" is a posture of heart that simply holds an awareness of need. It is not spiritual greed, which only seeks to consume with no desire to give. These are people who want every impartation and blessing under the sun (which is a good thing) but they fail to realise that with everything we receive, there is also a responsibility that comes with it—to use what we have been given. This is like the good servant who took what he was given and through wise stewardship brought about an increase. Spiritual greed takes the blessings and buries them in the ground, forgetting that we are blessed to be a blessing.

The purpose of blessing is twofold. First, it is to reveal His love and goodness to us personally. And second, it is to transform us into His likeness, making us a living revelation of His love and goodness to others.

God blesses us and then transforms us into that very blessing to carry out to the world. Why do you think so many who have powerful healing ministries have experienced a significant healing in their life at some point? It is not a rule, but history shows that many people who moved in a powerful anointing of healing were blessed with a healing in their own life and, through wise stewardship, transformed it into a blessing of healing to so many others. Every blessing we receive comes with an opportunity to become a transformed-being for the sake of His kingdom on the earth.

Those who are not poor in spirit will moan over the size of the blessing, but the wise will take what they have been given and run with it. I took a healing from hay fever and through stewardship, increased what was given to me. A healing from hay fever is not considered that dramatic if you were to compare it to a terminal illness or physical disability being healed. But I did not care about that; it was still an impossibility being made possible. It is just as impossible to make a speck of dust disappear as it is to make a skyscraper disappear. If you allow yourself to see the fullness of His Spirit that is made available to us in every single miracle, then you will be the "poor in spirit" who will inherit the Kingdom that Jesus spoke of. Position yourself to see His presence flow through you by taking healing to those who need a miracle. It is as simple as that. You will find these people in your workplace, school, university, grocery store, on the street—anywhere in your everyday life. Placing yourself in a situation where you need His presence to show up puts you in the perfect place to see Him move.

Smith Wigglesworth understood this.

If the Spirit of God does not move me, I move the Spirit.[4]

It was not arrogance; it was a deep trust in his relationship with the Father where Smith knew he could position himself to place such a demand on God's goodness, that the Father simply could not resist. The fact is, the Father is incredibly attracted to faith.

Selah.

End Notes

1. Author's paraphrase based on Est. 4:14.
2. See Rom. 12:2.
3. See Luke 4:18.
4. Liardon, Roberts. *God's Generals*, p. 216.

ACTIVATION

In your daily life, how can you better position yourself to see the Holy Spirit released through you to the world around you?

Think of three different ways that you would be able to position yourself in such a way that places a demand on the goodness of God to heal.

As an example, consider the following:

• Choose to minister to a person in a setting that is outside of your comfort zone.

• Choose to ask God for a word of knowledge about a person that you are going to see who has a need of healing.

• Choose to minister to someone who has a need of healing at the supermarket while you are shopping and then refuse to leave until you do.

• Choose to go for a walk at a park or to a cafe whilst at the same time looking for a person who has need of healing to minister to. Determine not to head home until you have prayed for someone.

• Decide to pray for every person you buy coffee from for two weeks. If they don't need healing, pray a prayer of blessing over them. This helps build courage.

In His wisdom
The sun He made
To rise each morning
Declaring His raid
Reminding us of
The Son who came
Emptying hell's treasury
And removing the chains
His bride He freed
To glorious love
The sun rises each morning
Just for us
Over the mountain rays
Start to shine
Lest we forget
The sun's made to rise

"Sunrise"
by Josh Klinkenberg

CHAPTER

7

Stewarding the

Seed

J esus presented a parable to the disciples about a
seed.

> *The kingdom of heaven is like a mustard seed,*
> *which a man took and sowed in his field; and*
> *this is smaller than all other seeds, but when it*
> *is full grown, it is larger than the garden plants*
> *and becomes a tree, so that the birds of the air*
> *come and nest in its branches.*

Matthew 13:31-32

Oftentimes, when we pray for a "tree," for example,
the Lord answers by giving us seed. What if Jesus has
already answered every prayer you have ever prayed—
only in seed form, and He is expecting you to steward that

seed into full maturity? I am not saying this is definitely the case, but I do know this: the Lord answers more of our prayers than we realise, and we can easily miss it because we are looking for a "tree" when He has given us seed. Why does He do this? Because, the sowing and stewardship of that seed is the very thing that will cultivate the maturity in us to handle the fullness of the answer to our prayer.

Not long ago I met with a pastor who happened to have a really nice car. I was daydreaming with God thinking, "It would be nice, Father, to have a car like that. Could I have one?"

In return, He asked me a question: "Do you have the faith to pay for the tyres, the servicing, and the maintenance of such a nice car?"

In that moment, it was like He released a grace for me to be able see myself in complete honesty. I could "see" the maturity of my faith at that time could not trust Him for the money required to maintain such a car.

The Lord continued: "If I gave you that car right now, you would go bankrupt because you do not yet have the faith to maintain it."

That moment with the Lord amazed me because I always thought I was someone who had great faith. In fact, I have generally found it easy to believe God for just about anything. But in that moment I saw that in His mercy He did not give me the "tree" that I was asking for; instead, He gave me a seed that if stewarded correctly, would result in the full answer to that prayer. And, for the record, I am still growing my "Porsche" tree!

Although it is not about getting a flash car or nice "things," the lesson applies across the board. This simple faith lesson has allowed me to step deeper into a partnership with God that is resulting in a rapid growth in my own maturity, which in turn has enabled a greater release of answered prayer. At times God will withhold a blessing only because He sees that it will destroy us. So instead, He gives us a seed that He wants us to steward. In doing so, we develop the character and maturity needed to receive the very thing that He, in mercy had to withhold. God will not give us anything that will bring destruction. We are His children and He cares for our wellbeing.

That does not mean that He is going to spoil us rotten by doing everything we ask of Him. His will is that we would become mature friends who can reign with Him as co-heirs in His kingdom. As a good father, I do not let my 2-year-old daughter play with knives because I care for her wellbeing. Even if she is screaming her head off because she thinks she really needs it, I will not allow her to play with knives. But one day she will be mature enough to handle knives without my supervision.

So it is at times in the Kingdom. This is not a rule for everything we pray for, but it is a reality that is more common than perhaps we give credit for. We easily come to the conclusion that God has not answered our prayers, when in actual fact He has given His answer to us. We simply need to steward that thing into maturity. It is my conviction that God says "Yes!" more than we know.

Faith, the size of a mustard seed, is not meant to stay the size of a mustard seed. Jesus tells His disciples that if they had faith the size of a small mustard seed, they could command mountains to "move," and they would.[1] Jesus was talking to them about the size of their faith—it was very small. They were unable to cast a single demon out but they did not know why. When they asked Jesus, He began this parable by saying,

Because of the littleness of your faith.

Matthew 17:20

This seems a weird thing for Jesus to say especially when we read the next line and He says that faith, even the size of a mustard seed, would move mountains! He just told them that the reason they could not do what they were trying to do was because of the "littleness" of their faith and then He tells them that if they had faith the size of a mustard seed—the smallest of seeds—they would be able to do anything! It is a confusing Scripture when taken on its own like this. What did Jesus mean?

When we look back and see that just a short time earlier, Jesus was with the disciples[2] telling them that the Kingdom of heaven is like a mustard seed which needs to be sown in the field of our hearts and stewarded well so that it becomes a full grown tree. Between chapter 13 and 17, Jesus expected them to have stewarded this faith-seed in a way that caused it to grow.

Seeing that His disciples still had not understood this, Jesus gives them a key on how to steward the seed of deliverance in their lives.

This kind does not go out except by prayer and fasting.

Matthew 17:21

In that moment Jesus was neither praying nor was He fasting, and yet He still cast out the demon. Why? He was living a life of stewarding the seed of deliverance through His life. He spent time with the Father on the mountain, many times praying all night. He would often withdraw Himself from the crowds just to be alone with His Father. This type of life results in a seed being watered and nurtured.

It is not long before it becomes a tree big enough for all the birds of the air to come and nest in its branches.

And this is smaller than all other seeds, but when it is full grown, it is larger than the garden plants and becomes a tree, so that the birds of the air come and nest in its branches.

13:32

These birds, I believe, represent the angels. Stewarding the seed of your heart into a mature tree creates a place for the angelic realm to rest.

The ministry of healing is one of these seeds that needs to be tended in the garden of our heart. I prayed for a gift of healing on my life and God answered that prayer in seed form. Since then I have been stewarding that seed of healing to see it mature to the point where I can see that tree fully grown and it did not kill me. What I mean is that I can honestly say if I had seen those healing miracles that I was praying for back then in their fullness, it would have killed me. I would have just been another victim of one of the "three G's": the gold, the glory, or the girls.

The Lord is in the process of raising up a people who have the maturity to handle the fullness of the raw power that He wants to release. We have only scraped the surface in terms of what is going to be seen on the earth. There are countless people all over the world, both young and old, who have been faithfully stewarding the seed of the Kingdom in their hearts for years. In that stewardship a character is being formed that will enable these faithful ones to carry the flame they so desire to see.

Increase Our Faith

In Luke, the disciples finally figure out that the key to all this craziness they had witnessed was faith. So they come to Jesus with the request of all requests within the Kingdom. They said, "Lord, increase our faith!"[3] Jesus replies with the all too familiar story of the mustard seed, which again reiterates the importance of the parable in Matthew 13. But He goes on to share this amazing story, which at first seems like a total shift of focus. It sounds like He is talking about something completely different.

> *If you had faith like a mustard seed, you would say to this mulberry tree, "Be uprooted and be planted in the sea," and it would obey you. Which of you, having a slave plowing or tending sheep, will say to him when he has come in from the field, "Come immediately and sit down to eat"? But will he not say to him, "Prepare something for me to eat, and properly clothe yourself and serve me while I eat and drink; and afterward you may eat and drink"? He does not thank the slave because he did the things which were commanded, does he? So you too, when you do all the things which are commanded you, say, "We are unworthy slaves; we have done only that which we ought to have done."*

17:6-10

The disciples ask for Jesus to increase their faith and He comes back to them with a story about who is making dinner! We have to understand that when the disciples heard Him mention the mustard seed, they would have been thinking in context of Matthew 13 where they were first told about a seed that needed to be sown. In these few verses that seem strange, Jesus just gave them the

128

key to stewarding the seed of faith. He gave them the "how to" of Matthew 13.

It is interesting that Jesus uses plowing or tending sheep as the two works. Plowing represents breaking new ground or working the soil of peoples' hearts, whereas tending sheep represents taking care of His people. What Jesus says here is profound. After we have done everything that we are meant to do, after we have broken new ground in the Spirit, after we have ministered to hearts, after we have taken care of His people, fed the poor and clothed the needy, after we have prayed for the sick, and done all sorts of miracles, we do not come demanding of the Father to eat and drink. Instead, we first prepare a feast for Him. We clothe ourselves properly; we serve Him while He eats the fruit of our lips—praise and worship.

The key that Jesus reveals to us is profoundly simply: the way to increase our faith is to prepare a feast for Him—a feast of worship, adoration and love. The amazing thing is, in this feast we are not left hungry, because the Scripture says that afterwards we eat and drink. There are plenty of people who come before the Father wanting to be filled up and satisfied but are unwilling to prepare a feast for Him first and they wonder why they are never filled in the way that they know they need.

The best way to steward your seed of faith into a mighty tree is to serve the all-faithful One. When you hang out with the One who is full of faith, the natural result is that you too, become full of faith.

The way to increase in faith is to increase in intimacy. Any formula for more faith that exists outside of intimacy is a hoax. Don't waist your time with it.

The disciples came with a request that many of us can identify with: "Lord, increase our faith!"

Jesus says if you have faith the size of a mustard seed, you could grow that into a tree which would result in anything being possible. So here is how you steward that seed: prepare a feast of worship to the Father—bless Him, love on Him. Serve Him first and then be satisfied yourselves.[4]

Preparing a feast for the Father in this way protects us from the arrogance that we can so easily slip into when we begin to see the Spirit of God move in power through us.

When you serve somebody, you catch what they carry. The disciples served Jesus and they caught what He carried. Stephen and Phillip served the disciples and they caught that same thing. So what would it look like for a generation to serve the One who is faithful—that is, the One who is full of faith? What kind of faith would we catch? What kind of impossibilities would suddenly cease to exist?

I encourage you today to make a feast of worship to Him your daily priority. When all the busyness of work and ministry is finished for the day and you feel tired and spent, come before Him and prepare for Him a feast. May we be those who see with our own eyes the results of raw faith displayed across the earth!

End Notes

1. Matt. 17:20.
2. 13:31-32.
3. Luke 17:5.
4. See Rom. 12:3.

ASSIGNMENT 3

Take a moment to remember and reflect upon the miracles you have seen in your life. Whether it's been a miracle of healing, provision, salvation, joy, emotional healing, deliverance, or anything else, it is important that we continue to remind ourselves of these moments.

Act 1: Miracle Journal

One of the most enjoyable things I get to do is write in my miracle journal. I love to remember, in detail, what I got to see the Lord do. I love knowing that I am writing to my grandchildren and to their children's children. I love being alone with the Father sharing about the memories we have created together.

Today is the day you start your very own miracle journal! If you have one already that's great; let's add to it. If this is your first one, go to the store and purchase a nice journal, one that you can pass on to your children and they on to theirs.

Act 2: Faithful Scribe

One of the things that we can do to steward our seed well is to become a faithful scribe. Write down the miracles you remember. Write as much detail as possible. Write about how you felt in those moments. Write down the miracles you saw from the earlier activations in this book. Include how you felt when you were praying for those people. Were you nervous, excited, anxious, afraid, scared, or bold? It's important that we can look back and remember what the Lord did through our weakness and through our strength.

THE ART OF HEALING

You may have only seen one or two miracles in your life, or you may have seen dozens, even hundreds. For some, it will take a while to remember these moments and that is totally fine! Take as much time as you need.

Act 3: Miracles are Seeds

These miracles are seeds in your life that are to be planted in the soil of your heart to grow and produce more fruit. From the testimonies you have written, ask the Lord to set up divine appointments over the next week where you can steward this seed and bring increase. You will find that He will bring people across your path who have a need in the same area that you have seen breakthrough in. These are the ones whom He has set aside for you to bless!

As you release breakthrough to these ones that He brings across your path, you will see your seed begin to grow and increase, bringing in even more seed to be stewarded and more fruit to be enjoyed!

Act 4: Taking Possession

Pray this prayer below and enjoy taking possession of your Promised Land!

Father, I thank You for all the times You have blessed me and moved through me. Remembering what You have done in me and through me, I can see that You have given me breakthrough in these areas [mention them here].

I ask that You would help me to steward

these seeds in my life into fullness. Would You set up divine appointments throughout this week where I get the chance to extend these boundaries and bring increase to these seeds?

I ask for courage and boldness, Father, to take these opportunities as I recognise them. Amen.

I know that
You're my Healer
I know that
You're my friend
I know now that
You love me
Just the way I am
Every time I hear You
I become undone
You've wrecked me
With Your goodness, God
You've wrecked me
With Your love

"How I Need You"
by Josh Klinkenberg

8

Increasing the

Inheritance

God is moving His church from glory to glory.[1] One of my all-time favourite things to do is to study past revivals and revivalists. I love to read and hear about what these amazing men and women of God did as they believed God for the impossible. They lived a life that earned them titles from their peers, such as, "lunatic," "heretic," "madmen," and even "devil possessed!" But their heavenly titles were, "Apostles of Faith," "Generals of Love," "Sons and Daughters of the Most High." With spiritual hindsight we see their lives with a greater perspective. What was the mysterious future to the revivalists of old is to us the revealed past.

We see how God used these hungry hearts to uncover a view of heaven that had been previously hidden from His people. I believe this is an essential part of every believer's "training in the Spirit." To know what He has done, opens the door to what He is *going* to do. From these stories I have learned keys, principles, and Kingdom standards that have—and are—shaping my life and ministry today.

There is one thing that we must keep in mind when looking into the history books of heaven on earth and that is this: We cannot develop our complete theology as we look at church history, especially in the area of healing. Why? Because those revivalists were breaking ground that we now are called to build on! To look at standards set in the past and aim for those today would be like a runner crossing the starting line and celebrating it as if he had just crossed the finish line, when in reality, he still had to cover the full 100-meters of ground he was given. To hit standards that were set in the past is a good start; but ultimately, we are called to go further! Reviewing the faith heroes of the past allows us to learn valuable keys, receive revelation, and pick up treasure beyond value. But we must always remember that God is moving His church from glory to glory.

I have heard a number of people try to explain that even in the great healing revivals of the past, not everyone was healed—as if to say, that standard is an acceptable premise for why everyone is not healed today. This is an incredibly flawed way to develop theology on healing. Again, we are not trying to merely achieve what has already been done in the past; we are called to build upon it. Standards of the past were never intended to be a limit to try to reach; they were intended to be a launching pad from where we start. Jesus is our God-given example and we must always follow Him rather than lowering our standards to make the God of impossibilities fit into our logic.

I believe the reason these amazing men and women

of the past did not experience the manifestation of every person receiving healing in their meetings is because that ground takes more than one generation to possess. The revivalists of the past were called to hand us the rights to territory that we were meant to increase, and in turn, we will hand this off to our children as their inheritance that would continue to bring yet more increase. The biblical way is that fathers fight for land and take it so their children can fully possess it.

These spiritual fathers and mothers of the past were not handing us boundaries to stay within; they were handing us markers from where to begin. What they experienced—in all of its greatness—was meant to be our starting point, but it was definitely not intended to be the ultimate destination.

Anything we are given in the Kingdom we are called to steward well in order to bring increase. In Matthew 25 and Luke 19, Jesus teaches the parable of the talents. He taught that wise servants were those who stewarded well what they were given and thereby produced substantial increase. By contrast, Jesus also spoke of the foolish servant who chose to bury his talent, refusing to even invest it. It is interesting to note how Jesus ends the story.

To everyone who has, more shall be given.

Luke 19:26

We have been given an inheritance in the area of healing. Let us be faithful stewards and bring increase with this gift. When it comes to increase in the Kingdom, it really is like the story in this parable where we are faithful with a small, seemingly insignificant amount, and the next thing we know, we are given a city to rule!

In faith we are called to take what has been handed to us through our fathers and mothers before us. Sure, we might not "feel" as anointed as our forefathers, but if "Elijah was just a man,"[2] then, so were these giants of the Kingdom. It is not about *feeling* as anointed as what we think they felt; it is about claiming what is rightfully ours in *faith*. The key word is "faith," not "feel."

Some of the most incredible miracles I have seen at the end of my own hands have been those times when I least "felt" like anything was going to happen. It is during such times I remember that the truth of His kingdom in me is not a feeling, but a fact I take by faith. His power in and through me is still present even when I do not feel like it is.

We all know that at times our feelings deceive us. We have all watched a movie that made us cry or felt really sad, or even really angry because of something bad that went on, when in reality, nothing bad actually happened! In most cases the only bad thing that happened was we had to actually pay to watch some of these films!

The more I learn to trust in truth the more my feelings come into alignment with it. To rely on feelings instead of faith only serves to rob those around you of what you really carry inside.

Faith requires an action. To claim what was given to us in faith requires that we live out a life that is built upon that belief. We cannot see what these men and women of old saw in the Spirit unless we too, are willing to act upon what they gave us as our inheritance. I shared earlier that I used to pray and pray, "God, use me to heal the sick!" and how after a number of months, He answered with profound simplicity and said, "Don't you think it would be a good idea to actually pray for a sick person?" In that moment, I felt Him lovingly say, "Stop praying for something you already have."

Many have expressed a desire to see the dead raised.

But, in order for that to happen, guess what we have to do? We have to command a dead person to rise up! If you have not had the chance to command a dead person to rise, then I can almost guarantee that you would not have seen a dead person rise. But does that mean that you do not have the ability to raise the dead? Selah.

The Lord puts it like this through His prophet Isaiah:

> *What more was there to do for my vineyard that I have not done in it? Why, when I expected it to produce good grapes did it produce worthless ones?*

> Isaiah 5:4

This chapter of Isaiah is a fascinating prophetic word. It is the story of the Lord planting a vineyard. He provided everything needed to ensure it has the best possible conditions to produce good fruit. He removed the rocks, tended the ground, planted the best vine, made a wine vat, and even placed a lookout tower in the middle of the vineyard. Then He patiently waited for the vineyard to yield a good crop. But what He received instead was worthless grapes.

He asks His people this question: "What more was there to do for My vineyard that I have not done in it?" In other words, "Was there something I did not do which I should have done? Tell me what I missed?" The fact is, the Lord knew—and His people knew—there was nothing more He could have done. The vineyard had been given everything it needed.

This is exactly the question I hear echoing through the Spirit realm to so many believers today who are waiting for God to do what has already been done! So many people resort to excuses, such as, "If God wanted to heal them, they would have lived. . . ." or, "If God wants

139

them healed He will do it." But God is asking this question in reply, "Was there something I missed? My Son died on the cross and made full provision. What more is there to do that I have not already done?" That is why He has an expectation that we will produce good fruit because He has given us everything we need in order to produce the best fruit imaginable!

We see another amazing key further on in this same chapter. The prophet Isaiah reveals in this word to Israel a key that will keep us in possession of the land we have been given.

> *They do not pay attention to the deeds of the Lord, nor do they consider the work of His hands. Therefore My people go into exile for their lack of knowledge; and their honourable men are famished, and their multitude is parched with thirst.*
>
> vs. 12-13

Having an awareness of what He has done and meditating on His works keeps us in possession of the land He has given us. To "pay attention to the deeds of the Lord" is having an awareness of what He is doing, and to "consider the works of His hands" is meditation—dwelling on that which He has already done. Failing to live with these two postures causes us to "go into exile."

The point of what God is saying is to stay aware of His presence. Do whatever you can to remind yourself continually in order to be conscious of His Spirit and of just how close and present He really is. Keeping a mindful awareness, and staying attentive to Him, will ensure that we see all He does and hear all He is saying, which increases the depth of our intimate relationship moment by moment. The journey of a thousand miles starts with one step. Every relationship is a journey and intimacy is increased one step at a time. Meditating on what you have seen Him do in the past will enlarge your ability to see and hear Him in the present.

Regularly dwell on the miracles you have heard and seen. Dwell on the fact that the impossible happened through those miracles. If you have prayed for someone and seen them healed, make sure the impact of that miracle really hits you. It is too easy to get conditioned or desensitised to God working the miraculous, but we never want to allow this way of thinking to rob us of the depth of glory that is released every time the Lord does something. Instead, meditate on every single miraculous work until you are once again filled with awe and amazement. Then, and only then, have you begun to truly see what happened when He showed up. In this way, you position yourself to see those very works be reproduced through you.

Remember:

*The testimony of Jesus **is** the spirit of prophecy.*

Revelation 19:10, emphasis added

Dwelling on these testimonies of Jesus prophesies the release of them again through us.

End Notes

1. 2 Cor. 3:18.
2. James 5:17.

ASSIGNMENT 4

This assignment is designed to stretch you and push you even further out of your comfort zone.

❖ *Release healing over 5 people within the next week in a creative way.*

What we are going to do this time is release healing to 5 people in a way that does not involve the conventional way of "praying for the sick."

Instead, your prayer is going to look and sound like something completely different. It could take the form of a painting, a song, or a poem. It could be that you simply place your hand on the person without saying anything, and then after a moment, ask them to test it out. There are hundreds of creative ways to release the Kingdom and I want you to explore a few of these this week.

❖ *Be creative, jump out of the box, jump over the "chicken line," and see impossibilities bow their knee to Jesus as the love of God is released through you in a creative way!*

Remember to write the testimonies down in your miracle journal.

Like a flooding river
Like a heavy rain
Fill me on the inside
With Your love again
Let Your Spirit light shine
The darkness away
That the world
Would see You
Lifted up in me

"Flood Me"
by Josh Klinkenberg

9

Contending Versus Striving

ontending and striving are two very different things. One ends in victory and the other ends in defeat. Jesus said:

Repent, for the kingdom of heaven is at hand.

Matthew 3:2

As you may know, the word "repent" means to change the way we think. Jesus was telling people to change the way they think and to return to God's way of thinking. Why was He saying this? The culture to which Jesus was speaking was ruled by a very strict and demanding religious system. Woven into it all was a deep-rooted mindset that God was impersonal, distant and far off. Their whole way of life was based around rigorous religious requirements that believed in a distant God who needed to be bribed into responding to their needs through pious works and rituals.

Sadly, some Christians today have the same mindset. But Jesus' message is clear, "Repent! Change the way you think!" What do we need to change? We need to take to heart that the Kingdom is near, not far off; it's right here within arms' reach!

The difference between contending and striving is founded upon this understanding that the Kingdom of heaven is here in our midst. Striving through human efforts, attempts to get some far off, distant god to come close to us through "good works." This mindset suggests we needed to bribe God into loving His beloved. But we already know He loves us! Contending, on the other hand, recognises that the Kingdom is already here among us and acts on pursuing the fullness of that fact in order to see it as a manifested reality. Contending is placing a demand on the promises of God.

Contending does not stop at just "praying in" the promises of God; it chases them down with intentional and pro-active action. Contending takes God at His Word and places a demand on what He has promised. Jesus said, "The kingdom of heaven is at hand." Contending is the act of putting a demand on that promise to see it come into the fullness that He so desires! Every time I pray for the sick I am actively pursuing the fullness that was promised. Every time you act on what God has promised, you are actively contending for the fullness of that promise to be made manifest. That is what contending looks like. Contending is the part of faith that pulls the reality of heaven into the earth.

Jesus provided everything we needed by His death on the cross and unlocked all the promises of God for us.

*Blessed be the God and Father of our Lord Jesus Christ, who has blessed us with **every** spiritual blessing in the heavenly places in Christ.*

Ephesians 1:3, emphasis added

Our position to contend for the fullness promised must be built upon this foundation. Yet, we must realise that while we have been given these promises, it does not necessarily mean we fully possess them. Contending is the act of taking possession of what God has already given us. Just as Abraham was given the Land of Israel hundreds of years before the Israelites took possession of it, we too, have not yet taken possession of all we have been promised.

From the cross, Jesus said, "It is finished."[1] So we know that everything that needed to be done has been done. Every spiritual blessing has been given to us through Christ Jesus. In other words, we have been given everything. The only reason we are not seeing the manifest evidence of this is because we have not yet taken possession of all that we have been given.

How does this relate to healing? When we do not see every sick person healed, does that mean that God does not want every sick person healed? Or, could it signify that we simply have not yet taken full possession of our Promised Land—healing? One of the most common reasons people choose to believe that God's heart is not to heal everyone is because they have not seen everyone healed that was prayed for. In choosing to believe this, we willingly leave a part of the Promised Land of healing uninhabited. Jesus did not live like this and neither should we.

One of the greatest joys in taking possession of this particular portion of the Promised Land is the route in how we get there. It is quite simple, really. We take possession of healing by healing the sick! We take possession of deliverance by casting out demons. We take possession of raising the dead by raising the dead!

On the other hand, "striving" prays for God to give us something that He has already given. It actually seeks ways to earn what He already paid for. Whereas, "contending" partners with what God said is already ours. It is the act of us reaching out and taking hold of the Kingdom that is presently at hand.

Imagine a rich man decides to entrust a large portion of his wealth to two of His most trusted friends. He sends his son to sort out the legalities and pay all the fees involved. Once it is all taken care of, the rich man calls the two friends in to see him. He shares with them that he has given them more money than they could possibly spend in their lifetime. He lets them know that it is all sitting in an account in his son's name and that they have full access to it.

A number of months pass and one day, the rich man sees both of his friends again. As he meets with the first friend, they get to chatting about life and all that has been going on. This friend shares about those in his life that were going through a really hard time. The friend had family members who were struggling financially and some who were even in a rough place with their health. But with excitement in his voice, the rich man's friend went on to share how he was able to use some of the money to help these ones in need. He made sure they were blessed and well taken care of. He used the wealth he had been given to see his family and those he came into contact with fully restored to wholeness and health. The rich man and his friend laughed with enjoyment as they shared stories of lives they had seen changed because of the wealth they had access too.

Later that day, the rich man found himself sitting with the other friend to whom he had given a great portion of his wealth. Again, the conversation drifted towards life and those his friend loved. His friend began to ask the rich man if he was able to pay off the debt his family owed. This friend also had loved ones' with health needs, so he asked the rich man if he was willing to pay for their health care costs. His friend began to beg the rich man for the money needed to rectify these problems. The rich man wept with his friend and held him close, comforting him. The rich man said to his friend, "I have already given you everything I have." This friend went away sad because he felt like there was nothing he could do. He thought the rich man would surely sort out all the problems that were in front of him, not realising that indeed, he already had.

Contending acts on the fact that the Father has given us everything in His Son. Striving begs the Father to do what, through Christ, we have already been given the authority to do ourselves.

Striving–type prayers are ultimately rooted in doubt and unbelief. Striving prays in a way that does not acknowledge the life that Christ has purchased for us because it still addresses God as if He is distant and far off. Striving forgets that His is Immanuel, God *with* us.

When it comes to healing, striving prays like this: "God, if it is Your will, would You please heal this person? If You heal them, God, all these other people will see—the doctors, the family members, they will all see—and they will come to hear about You . . ."

Whereas, contending-type prayers are rooted in faith and find their hope in God's faithfulness. These types of prayers believe, and act upon the truth of what God has said. Contending believes that His kingdom is at hand and it reaches out into the unknown to grab hold of it.

149

Again, in regards to healing, contending sounds like this: "In the name of Jesus, I say, be healed!"

Notice the first type of prayer begs God to heal someone whom He already healed 2,000 years ago in Christ. The second type of prayer steps into the life and authority He has given to us as believers. We never see Jesus, or even the disciples, praying a striving-type of prayer when they were faced with healing the sick. They simply commanded them to be well!

Prayer must lead to action. Faith must be outworked in deeds.[2] The temptation to move from contending into striving happens when we do not position ourselves to see our prayers answered. It is essential that we experience answered prayer. Jesus lived a life filled with answered prayer. In fact, He lived in such a way where every prayer He prayed was answered! And it is His desire for us to live the same way. For this is where we find the kind of joy that gives us strength to press on. Answered prayer is where we really see who God is and what He is like. It also enables us to keep our heart pure and filled with a joyful awareness of how close the Kingdom is on a continual basis.

Jesus spoke of this joy to His disciples.

These things I have spoken to you so that My joy may be in you, and that your joy may be made full.

John 15:11

What things had He spoken to His disciples about? He had just been talking about the results of abiding in Him:

I am the vine, you are the branches; he who abides in Me and I in him, he bears much fruit, for apart from Me you can do nothing.

v. 5

If you abide in Me and My words abide in you, ask whatever you wish, and it will be done for you. My Father is glorified by this, that you bear much fruit, and so prove to be My disciples.

vs. 7-8

Fullness of joy is found in answered prayer. Answered prayer is locked up in abiding in Him. It is from the position of "abiding" in Jesus that we are able to request whatever we wish in order that the Father would be glorified by the fruit our lives produce. In this way we prove that we are His disciples. As we abide in Him, we are positioning ourselves in a depth of oneness with the Father that allows us to see every request we make granted. And therein we unlock the secret of the fullness of joy.

As you have already read, part of my journey of desiring that God would use me to heal the sick is how He told me I needed to go and actually pray for the sick. As I followed through with this, I was able to see that God had actually answered this prayer of mine. And in this journey, I have also met others who are in the same place of asking God but have not yet seen His answer because they have not yet moved into that place to believe God and take action.

Jesus was very clear about His intentions as we bring Him requests:

If you ask anything in My name, I will do it.

John 14:14

So let us do that right now and ask the Lord for an ability to move in the gift of healing.

Pray this with me:

> *Jesus, I believe You when You say that if I ask anything of the Father in Your name, You will give it to me. So Father, I am asking right now for an ability to move in the gift of healing and the working of miracles. I ask that You would use my hands as Your own. May these hands of mine be used to set people free from sickness and disease. May my words be used to set people free from bondage and oppression. Father, I ask that the supernatural would take place in my everyday life—through my hands, my words, my relationships, and my actions. I am asking for an ability to move in the fullness of all that which You did for me through the resurrection of Jesus. I ask You for courage and boldness to fill my being right now, and I also ask for eyes to see and ears to hear every opportunity You give me to release healing as I go about my daily life. Thank You for Your promises. I believe You!*

Now, I want to encourage you to take action and discover just how fully the Father has answered that prayer! Heal the sick, cast out demons, raise the dead, and see the Kingdom released all around you!

Remember that you carry the King inside of you, and you also carry the King's domain—His kingdom. Life and healing is His domain and they are far superior to anything the enemy offers. When someone you meet is sick, it is the equivalent of the enemy bringing a knife to an atomic bomb fight! There is just no comparison between the two.

Remain in an awareness of the fact that you carry an all-powerful King and His all-powerful Kingdom. Release the King and His kingdom wherever you go, and watch what happens! His great joy will energise and fill you.

End Notes

1. See John 19:30.
2. James 2:26.

ASSIGNMENT 5

On a piece of paper that fits inside your Bible, write down a list of 5 to 10 specific conditions that you would like to personally see healed as you minister to others. This is a great way to work with the Lord. When we are clear about what we would really like to see breakthrough in, it gives Him the opportunity to really bless us by working with us and through us to see that happen.

• Step 1: Write down 5 to 10 specific conditions that you would like to see healed at the end of your own hands.

• Step 2: Place this piece of paper inside your Bible or somewhere you will see it regularly (i.e., on the refrigerator).

• Step 3: Ask the Lord to set you up with opportunities over the coming days and weeks to see breakthrough in these conditions.

• Step 4: Ask the Lord: "Is there anything I can do to position myself in a more effective way to see these conditions healed?"

You bring beauty
Out of the broken
You turn mountains
Into fields of rest
You call the lame to dance
In freedom
You are Father
To the forgotten
Making a way
For man to find
Life so contagious
The dead are rising
Transforming darkness
Into glorious light

"Mountains"
by Josh Klinkenberg

10

Common Cases

Against Healing

I want to explore a few of the most common belief systems and questions that are often used to build a case against God's heart to heal. Please understand that as you read this chapter I did not write these things out of the need to form an argument to defend healing. Instead, these are simply the answers I have found on my journey to settle the many questions that were in my own heart. The thoughts I share are a result of conversations with the Lord that were brought about through the questions I began to ask Him. I believe that allowing for mystery in your relationship with God is incredibly important. If we do not, then we automatically set the depth that we are willing to go with Him.

As I mentioned earlier, one of my favourite quotes is from Bill Johnson:

> *I will not sacrifice my knowledge of the goodness of God on the altar of human reasoning so I can have an explanation for a seemingly unanswered prayer.*

It is arrogance to believe we can ever fully understand God. But at different times in our journey we have crossed paths with a belief system where the mysteries of God's ways are an excuse to not question Him about the really tough issues of life. This is sad because it robs us of a depth of intimacy that the Father desires to share with us. What we began to encounter as we voiced the questions of our heart was an implication that we, as believers, were not allowed to ask these difficult questions and that we just needed to settle for the mystery of it all. At first, this sounds noble. But actually, when you are in the midst of a life-and-death storm, it is an incredibly cruel position for an all-loving Father to expect His children to have. It was a huge relief to us to discover that this is not His default expectation of us.

What I have come to learn is that there is a big difference between not asking a question and not receiving an answer. I have found that many people use the term "mystery" as the excuse to not ask God the hard questions in the first place. But the fact is, we have a promise that the Holy Spirit will be our Teacher and that He will lead us into all truth. Unfortunately, in our culture, the reason people often do not have an answer is because they have not heard their favourite speaker give one. Selah.

We need to relearn the art of asking the Holy Spirit questions. I am not afraid to ask God the tough questions and He is definitely not afraid to hear or answer them. When He gives me an answer, I am able to stand on it in full confidence. If He chooses to say that He is not going to give an answer, then—and only then—am I okay with mystery. Remember, Scripture says:

> *You do not have because you do not ask.*
>
> James 4:2

I know from my own journey that in many of us there is a constant, internal battle being fought: a war between faith and unbelief. It is often a war between our head and our heart where we have been intellectually indoctrinated with an incorrect belief system about how God works. But then He manifests Himself, and in the most unintelligible and illogical way, He completely opposes our belief system with the miraculous.

For example, it makes perfect sense in the Kingdom to destroy depression with an abundance of ridiculous laughter where the "patient" is left rolling around on the floor in a most undignified way. To the one who has been brought up with a belief system that the Holy Spirit is a Gentleman, that He is clean, tidy, controlled, and quiet in the way He works, such a seemingly outrageous demonstration of His presence provides a hurdle for them to continue on in relationship with Him whilst still holding on to that belief system.

In regards to healing, many people have inherited a belief system that acknowledges God heals, but only a select few. To jump into the fullness of the Kingdom in the healing arena we need to be willing to accept that it is God's will for *everyone* to be healed. Holding to this truth can be extremely offensive these days. Trust me, I know! It took me two long years to walk through a mountain of offence in this area because of what had happened in the life of my son.

It helps to remember that we are called to bring

this present reality into alignment with the reality of the Kingdom. Just because there are things that are out of alignment does not mean they are God's will. His will is to bring all that is out of alignment back into alignment with heaven.

We have to understand that healing is so much a part of salvation that to say God does not want everyone healed is to say that He does not want everyone saved. We know this is not true because the Scriptures clearly communicate God's will about each and every person.

> *The Lord is not slow about His promise, as some count slowness, but is patient toward you, not wishing for any to perish but for **all** to come to repentance.*
>
> 2 Peter 3:9, emphasis added

God made us spirit, soul, and body, which means He is interested in all three parts of the person. He does not want to heal one part and leave another tortured in some way.

God is looking for a people who will possess the wholeness of salvation in spirit, soul and body. We, as a group of believers, have come to the place now where we are able to accept that God wants us whole in spirit and soul. But, for some reason, we still struggle to believe that He also wants to see wholeness in our bodies. For too long, the church has devalued the physical body of a person. And yet, it is our bodies that are the temple of the Holy Spirit.[1] God does not despise our physical being. In fact, He wants to use our bodies to display His glory on the earth.

Healing is a gift that is meant to lead us into our God-given destiny of divine health. It is His desire that we would live in divine health. Not only that, it is possible to carry it in such a way that every person who comes into contact with you in some tangible way will step into that same atmosphere of divine health. God has done this in the lives of a few here and there, but His heart is that it would be the reality of His entire body.

I am becoming so used to living in an atmosphere of life, that oftentimes I can tell when sickness is present in a person because it feels like I am breathing something in that I should not be. It feels like the air in the room actually changes. Because of this I do not often get sick and I am able to recognize—and rebuke—sickness before it is able to affect me. When people see that sickness does not affect your body and you are in good health, they will want to know how. You will be a shining light illuminating the path for people to meet a Saviour who does not torture them, but He nurtures them, cares for them, protects them, and blesses them. This is a Saviour who finds delight in displaying His glory through the whole person—spirit and soul and body.

> *Wherever He entered villages, or cities, or countryside, they were laying the sick in the marketplaces, and imploring Him that they might just touch the fringe of His cloak; and as many as touched it were being cured.*
>
> Mark 6:56

Think about that: every person who even touched Jesus' clothes was completely healed. It puzzles me how we, as believers, go from this display of healing to the belief that God allows sickness.

Mark chapter six reveals an astonishing fact as Jesus walks with His disciples to His hometown of Nazareth.

> *Jesus went out from there and came into His*

hometown; and His disciples followed Him. When the Sabbath came, He began to teach in the synagogue; and the many listeners were astonished, saying, "Where did this man get these things, and what is this wisdom given to Him, and such miracles as these performed by His hands? Is not this the carpenter, the son of Mary, and brother of James and Joses and Judas and Simon? Are not His sisters here with us?" And they took offence at Him. Jesus said to them, "A prophet is not without honour except in his hometown and among his own relatives and in his own household." And He could do no miracle there except that He laid His hands on a few sick people and healed them.

Mark 6:1-5

Just prior to this, a woman was healed of a 12-year physical issue as she simply touched Jesus' clothes, and a young girl was raised up from the dead.[2] Jesus was operating in phenomenal power! Yet when He came to Nazareth, the miracles stopped. Why is this? Clearly Jesus had come to His own hometown with a desire to heal all who needed healing. His will had not changed. So, what was different? The people in Nazareth were offended by Him. Intellectually, they just could not work out how Jesus was doing what He was doing. These are the same people who grew up with Him and they felt like they knew who He was. For Jesus to return home and teach the mysteries of God and display amazing supernatural miracles just did not make sense to their humanistic reasoning; it caused them to take offence.

This story ends with perhaps one of the most haunting verses in Scripture:

And He wondered at their unbelief.

v. 6

162

Jesus, the Son of the Living God, is standing before the people of His hometown performing all kinds of miracles, but their reasoning ended with the conclusion that they could not accept what they saw and heard because they could not understand it; and so, they were offended. From that time on, all Jesus could do in His hometown was "lay His hands on a few sick people and heal them." Their humanistic reasoning prohibited them from receiving God's full intentions at that time.

The conclusion that God *allows* sickness is the result of an effort to make sense of heavenly things with earthly understanding. We have such a culture of suspicion today where we have taught ourselves to actually be like "doubting Thomas"—we need to touch His hands and His side before we will believe. This way of thinking says, "I need to *see* in order to *believe*." Whereas the Kingdom says, "Believe and you will see." Like the Nazarenes, people are often offended at the way Jesus operates because they cannot logically work it out. With the offence they create a culture that limits Jesus to only heal a few sick people, when, in fact, His true nature is to heal and renew all who come to Him.

Have you ever wondered what Jesus really wanted to do in His hometown the day He visited? Consider what would have happened if the people of Nazareth had received Him with faith. If "healing a few sick people" was what Jesus was limited to, imagine what would have happened if the people received Him with a child-like faith and expectancy? What stories would we be reading about?

Did you know that healing is only the beginning of what God wants to do? I believe He wants to start with healing, but what He really wants to do is release complete renewal and transformation. God, the Creator of the universe, makes all things new! He will often initiate this process by healing, then renew and transform us, and then release that same process through us to see all creation restored and renewed as well.

If only the Nazarenes had not been offended that day we could have been reading about one of the greatest revivals of all time. We could be reading about miracles that had never been seen before in history. We could be reading testimonies about one of the few times Jesus was amazed at the extraordinary faith of men and woman. But, what we have instead is one of the few times Jesus was in awe and wonder at man's unbelief. If the people of Nazareth had not taken offence, we could have been learning from their success in faith to believe God for something that had never been done before on the earth. Instead, we are left to learn from their failure because of unbelief. Selah.

What is it you want to leave those who come after you: a great success or a great failure? It is a blunt question I know, but the reality is people will learn powerful truths from how we live our lives. The question is, will they learn great truths from the great things we did or from the great things we could have done? It is a haunting question that will motivate us towards faith.

In this story, where we see Jesus limited by unbelief to what we would call today, "a good healing meeting," we see that His heart was to do much, much more than He was allowed to. This is a common problem we also see today: Jesus shows up in ways we may not like. We, in our "superior wisdom" cannot make sense of it and in our heart, we take offence at Him, most of the time unknowingly. We simply do not like the way He moves here or there so we write it off as, "that's not God," because it is outside of our understanding. With this offence in our heart, we find ourselves living in a "Nazareth" experience of His power. Rather than dealing with the offence, we instead create a theology to back up our life of seeing "only a few sick people get healed." This type of theology comes out in statements like, "Jesus only heals a few," or, "God allows sickness to teach people lessons."

This theology of powerlessness attempts to give sickness some kind of value or purpose where Jesus never did. The fact is, God does not give value to sickness and disease, only to healing and wholeness. Humanistic reasoning can cause us to create a theology based out of a "Nazareth"-encounter with Jesus, not realising that it was us who put the limits on His power, not Him!

There are two things in Scripture that caused Jesus to "wonder." One is faith, and the other is unbelief in the presence of miracles. I do not want to be that person who Jesus looks at in wonder because of unbelief! I want to be a person who, like the Roman soldier, blows Jesus away in amazement because of extraordinary faith.[3] I want to be that one who draws on the deep heart of God to do so much more than I could even ask or imagine—someone who not only talks about the "greater works," but also sees and experiences them.

Imagine a church that allows Jesus to move in any way that He would like to. Imagine a church that was so unoffended at Jesus that He could move in the full power that He so desires to. Imagine a church that did not have to make excuses for people who were not being healed—a church that walked in such friendship with Life Himself that anyone who even touched their clothes was completely healed and brought to life! Imagine a church that moves so freely in the miraculous, seeing every natural law broken with miracles that make no earthly sense whatsoever, that seeing only a few sick people healed when they go home is considered a quiet day.

This is who we are called to be! I am not talking about an institution. No, I am talking about the church! I am talking about a body of genuine believers who are the very house of God on the earth.

Unbelief has many different faces in the west. It commonly shows up in a way that says, "Jesus would not move like that because that does not make sense to me."

I love the testimony and illustration of the woman who was instantly healed of her twelve-year physical ailment just by touching Jesus' clothes. As Jesus felt power leave His body, He turned around to face her and makes this amazing statement:

> *Daughter, your faith has made you well; go in peace and be healed of your affliction.*
>
> Mark 5:34

Where it reads, "made you well," the Greek word used here is again that beautiful word, *sozo*. He literally told this woman, "Your faith has saved you, made you whole, delivered you, and healed you." Imagine having people healed as they simply touch your clothes! That would be so awesome. But then imagine having people completely saved, healed, delivered, and whole when they touch your clothes! That is a whole other level of evangelism right there! This is what happened to the woman in her encounter with Jesus.

That, right there, is the fullness of salvation that I have been talking about! We don't just carry one aspect of salvation; we carry the whole package! Salvation, healing, and deliverance were never meant to be three separate elements; rather, they are all part of one another. This woman went for her healing and received *sozo*—wholeness—in that moment.

And so it should be when people come to us! From here, let's look at several of the most common cases that seem to be used as evidences against God's heart to heal. These belief systems and questions are things that we have encountered in our own hearts. What I have written below has come out of conversations with the Father as I have grappled with the many questions I discovered in my heart in our journey together.

Case 1: Judgement and Justice

Interestingly, this is perhaps one of the most common cases I see that prevents the ministry of healing from flowing to and through the believer. I have encountered many people who are hindered in either moving in healing or receiving healing because they have an earthly view of judgement and/or justice. What we need instead is heaven's heart on the matter.

Many people have a subconscious mindset that sickness is God's judgement and is therefore justice for the wrong doings in their life. To believe that sickness is judgement means you believe that you deserve sickness, and therefore, you accept and receive it. Accepting sickness as a judgement creates a covenant with it that empowers it with authority to stay.

Before the atonement of Jesus, we were completely fused with sin, which meant that when the Lord poured out judgement on sin, people died. The heart of the Lord was never to kill people but to judge the thing that continued to facilitate separation. Because there was no separation between sin and man, our very nature had become sinful, meaning that if the Father had poured out judgement on sin, we would have surely died. But our heavenly Father, in His incredible mercy, saw a way to pour out the necessary judgement on the thing that

167

continued to facilitate separation, while at the same time, providing a way for His lost children to return home.

This is where Jesus takes centre stage! Our beloved Bridegroom came, and by the sacrifice of His blood, separated sin forever from man! His blood is so powerful that it is able to take what had been fused to us—that which had become our very nature—and separate it as far as the east is from the west! In doing this, God had fully judged sin and death while at the same time giving us freedom and life. The judgement that would have once killed us is now life to us! Although in our old nature we deserved everything we got, in our new nature, we don't! In Christ, we have been made completely new: we have a new nature; we are a new creation. Because of this, we no longer need to accept sickness or feel like we deserve it. To say that we deserve something that belongs only to our old nature is to say that the newness He has given us is not complete. We know this is not true; our newness in Christ is absolutely complete. You have been recreated in Him.

Justice has also become a controversial term in certain circles because there are so many strong opinions on the matter which do not marry with the rest of the gospel. So it is often a topic that is left unmentioned. God is indeed a God of justice and Scripture bears this truth.

> *Righteousness and justice are the foundation of Your throne; lovingkindness and truth go before You.*
>
> Psalm 89:14

Some translations read, "Justice and judgement are the foundation of Your throne." God's throne is actually founded upon righteousness, justice and judgement.

Often people forget that it was God's judgement to

send His Son. They often forget that it was while we were still dead in sin, His Son died for us![4] When people have a view that depicts God as an angry God, I often say, "Yep, God was just so angry that He sent His very own Son."

The most well-known and quoted verse in the Bible, John 3:16, is followed by these amazing words from Jesus Himself.

> *For God did not send the Son into the world to judge the world, but that the world might be saved through Him. He who believes in Him is not judged; he who does not believe has been judged already, because he has not believed in the name of the only begotten Son of God. This is the judgment, that the Light has come into the world.*

vs. 17-19

Jesus is the judgement of the Father. His judgement was to make a way for man to be released from the enemy's power over us by defeating sin and death once and for all! The word for "judgement" in these verses also can be translated "decide" or "decision." The word "saved" is again that beautiful word Greek sozo, "to save, heal, deliver, make whole." In other words, God did not send the Son into the world to decide for the world, but that the world might be saved, healed, delivered and made whole through Him. This verse shows us that God did not send His Son to make the decision of what was going to happen with the world, but rather so that man could make the decision for themselves. Why? Because before Jesus came to earth, we were dead to sin and the only choice was death. Now in Christ, we can choose life over death. Galatians 5:1 says this same thing:

> *It was for freedom that Christ set us free.*

He had no other motive for our freedom than freedom itself. He just wanted us to be free to choose for ourselves. Before Christ, we had only an illusion of freedom. We were slaves to sin and death. But now in Christ, we are no longer slaves, but friends!

As sons and daughters of His kingdom we need to see with an eternal, heavenly perspective. This is especially true when it comes to judgement and justice. Having an earthly or carnal view of these two attributes of the Kingdom will affect the way we prophesy, pray, and interact with each other, which ultimately affects the way history unfolds. For instance, some might say, this person has sin in their life so they are sick because of that. However, Jesus told His disciples, "Whomever you forgive, I will forgive."[5] So, who then, is responsible? The person who is sick? God? Or us?

What has God provided for those who commit sins?

> *The prayer offered in faith will restore the one who is sick, and the Lord will raise him up, and if he has committed sins, they will be forgiven him.*

James 5:15

We have been brought into the most amazing place in all of the earth's history! For thousands of years sin has been the very thing man has never been able to conquer. No matter how good any person was, they were still as dirty rags compared to the righteousness of God. Then Jesus comes along and not only opens the door that no man has ever been able to open, He also gives us the keys to open it for others! Jesus has given us every provision to deal with both sin and sickness.

Many believers have a judgement mindset where they have been conditioned to expect that bad things

170

happen to "bad" people, because, in earthly terms, that is justice. We are called to a higher way of thinking. In 1 Corinthians 3:3 Paul rebukes the church of Corinth for acting like mere humans. Isn't that crazy? We have to be careful as sons and daughters of the Most High that we do not reduce ourselves to thinking and acting like "mere humans." This is especially important when it comes to judgement and justice.

God created man in His image and we know that He has an incredible love for us. When a person who has been so messed up by the enemy becomes a slave to sin and sickness, the Father does not see this as justice. When that person no longer knows that they were designed and created to be a son or daughter of the King, it breaks His heart. He is not angry towards them; rather He is concerned for them and cares deeply for them. He wants them to feel loved. He wants to pull them close. In their bondage the devil wins. When a murderer is sent to the electric chair for judgement, the devil wins. This is not heavenly justice. For true justice, the devil has to lose. Why? Because satan is our true enemy—not the acts of humanity. Remember the Bible says:

> *Our struggle is **not** against flesh and blood, but against the rulers, against the powers, against the world forces of this darkness, against the spiritual forces of wickedness in the heavenly places.*

Ephesians 6:12, emphasis added

Every time an injustice happens it can always be traced back to the devil. He is the source of injustice. Whether it be murder, suicide, violence, abuse, theft or any other type of crime, they have a root which traces back to the enemy and his influence in a situation, or in a person's life and way of thinking. The Father is not angry at the one who was lied to; His anger is directed at satan, the father of lies.

In order for there to be true justice, the true enemy needs to suffer loss. If, at the end of the day, our true enemy has not suffered loss, then true justice has not been served. When we wage war on a person because they are a criminal, we fail to see the true enemy—the devil—who still gets off scott-free. For example, when a child is molested and has their innocence stolen, that child can grow up in deep sexual confusion. This abused, hurting person could then turn around and commit the same acts against another child just as it was done to them. Obviously, those who commit such actions will suffer consequences and they need serious rehabilitation and help. But treating that person like garbage and leaving them to rot lets the devil win in every way. One victim-turned-criminal gets shamed and hated for the rest of their life, while an abused child has been drafted by the enemy to repeat the cycle. The devil wins on so many levels.

Justice needs to involve our real enemy, suffering loss. It is he who must be held responsible and it is he who must pay back what he tried to steal, kill, or destroy.

As I said, there are definite consequences that are in place for good reason. If you commit murder, you will get locked up; if you steal from someone, you will be made to repay it. But in this, let us not forget who our true enemy really is.

The devil would rather that we stay focused on the person who offends, or the one who did the crime so that we do not ever affect his dark realm by releasing forgiveness, freedom, and adoption! The devil would much rather we target a person instead of him. This means he can continue his works of darkness with success! When we argue and pull each other down, we keep one another from our true destiny found only in an environment of love, honour, mercy, and forgiveness. Seeing the sick healed, the murderer forgiven, and the hated loved is true justice. When the devil loses someone that he has used for the sake of his kingdom of darkness, we begin to see true justice. When the devil's slaves are set free from their captivity, made sons of God and given an inheritance, then we start to see heavenly justice taking place here on earth!

When love wins, the enemy loses. The Father does not win when lives are ruined and suffering is left to run free. To say it is justice for people to suffer with sickness is like saying it is justice for a criminal's child to be sold into slavery.

God loves every person on this earth. Every person. True justice takes place when they encounter His love and find wholeness and acceptance in it.

We see in the book of Acts when the enemy took one of God's first Holy Spirit-filled champions, Stephen.[6] Even though Stephen gave his life willingly, there was still a demand for justice posted before the throne of God due to the spilling of his blood. What did God not do? He did not come kill all those involved in martyring Stephen, even though they deserved it. Why? Because such an action would have caused the devil to win.

Instead, God brought true justice by taking one of the devil's champions and making him one of the Kingdom's most influential voices in all of history. That man was Saul, who was renamed, "Paul." Saul was the enemy's tool in murdering anyone who preached Jesus. Surely if anyone deserved "justice" under the "eye-for-an-eye" Old Testament law, it was him.

However, God puts true justice on display when He

causes loss to the enemy by grabbing ahold of Saul's heart with His love. The Father invites this murderer into a relationship with Him, and then He goes on to use "Paul" to expand the Kingdom in such a way that it causes a knockout blow to the enemy's kingdom of darkness.

In the same way, it was not justice for Jesus to come and kill all those who did wrong, even when they believed they did it in His name. To those responsible for His own death, Jesus responded in this way:

Father, forgive them . . .

Why did He say that?

For they do not know what they are doing.

Luke 23:34

He knew that in forgiveness, true justice would be served and the true enemy would suffer loss. How? Forgiveness restores us to the person we are meant to be—pure, holy, blameless, and loved. Forgiveness restores the standard found in the Father's heart. The justice of God was that Jesus came to earth and took back a host of captives enslaved by the enemy, retrieving millions of His children who were eternally lost to separation, and brought them back into the abundant life of freedom and intimacy!

Justice is life for the dead, health for the sick, love for the hated, freedom for the bound, grace for the fallen, forgiveness for the sinner. This is what plunders hell and populates heaven. This is what causes the devil loss and grants Jesus gain. Never forget that the cost of true justice has to be at the enemy's expense, not man's.

174

Case 2: The Sovereignty of God

The sovereignty of God is an interesting subject, especially in light of healing. No doubt you have heard it used many times as an argument about God choosing to heal some, but not others. Hearing this viewpoint so often, I had to settle the issue in my own heart in order to continue on in the journey of healing. What I am discovering is God's sovereignty is not a case against His will to heal, but rather, a case *for* it! For us to understand our position and authority in the light of God's sovereignty, we have to look at what God, in His absolute sovereignty, chose to do. It was in His sovereignty that He entrusted us with the ability to steward His divine power in the earth.

It was in His amazing sovereignty that He decided to give us the authority to cast out demons, pick up deadly serpents, drink poison with no effect, and lay hands on the sick to see them recover.[7]

He gave us His authority over anything the enemy throws at us: serpents and snakes, sickness and disease, all principalities and authorities. What better way to "kick the devil's butt" than through His children—the very ones the devil is seeking to destroy.

It was in God's sovereignty that He chose to send His only Son to put an end to sin and afflictions of all kinds. In His sovereignty He won the victory over sin, sickness, and bondage, and then in His sovereignty, He chose us to enforce this victory throughout the whole earth. In His sovereignty He made us His sons and daughters and heirs of His kingdom. In His sovereignty He chose to place us in authority over all the works of the enemy, and even over this earth itself.

With that, it is impossible to point to the sovereignty of God as an excuse that leaves people in their sickness, bondage, and sin. To do so denies the very work of the cross, which provides full restoration and positions us perfectly in Him. What we are really saying when we use "God's sovereignty" to explain away sickness is this: "God can choose to do whatever He wants." This is true . . . He can choose to do whatever He wants. But what we also need to realise is that it was in this freedom of choice He *chose* to covenant Himself to us. And in this covenant, He chose to give us His Word of perfect wholeness. Just as in my marriage I am in covenant to my wife, I have the ability to do whatever I want, whenever I want. But in my covenant to my wife, I have chosen to *give* myself to her. In my freedom, I have chosen to place myself within a covenant relationship where I now say, "I will use my freedom to bless and benefit you." This is what God has chosen to do in His sovereignty. So yes, God can choose to do whatever He wants. But in His covenant to us, He has chosen to place Himself inside a relationship where He chooses to say, "I am going to use My freedom to love, to bless, and to benefit you."

The change from the Old Covenant to the New Covenant was a massive shift that affected everyone and everything. Let's look at one passage in Scripture that show perhaps one of the most significant changes for us as New Covenant sons and daughters.

> *So Jesus said to them again, "Peace be with you; as the Father has sent Me, I also send you." And when He had said this, He breathed on them and said to them, "Receive the Holy Spirit. If you forgive the sins of any, their sins have been forgiven them; if you retain the sins of any, they have been retained."*

John 20:21-23

This is perhaps one of the most powerful and mind-blowing verses in all of Scripture! If there is any Scripture in the Bible that needs a great big, "selah!" after it, for me, this would be it! The very thing that continued to facilitate the illusion of separation from the Father was sin. The devil was not a problem until we gave him authority through sin. Unfortunately, sin was the one thing that man was completely powerless to do anything about.

Why? Because a slave cannot set another slave free. In a world filled with slaves, there was not one free from sin who could come and set others free. It took Jesus, the only free person on earth to do that for us. This is absolutely amazing in and of itself. But then He goes one step further and invites us to share His forgiveness with everyone we meet—to see them released from their sin and brought into His forgiveness! Not only did He set us free from sin, but He also put us in a position of authority over it. He has put His Spirit within us, and in His Spirit is the very forgiveness that the Father released on the cross. With that forgiveness residing within us, He removes the very thing that continued to pull man away from the Father: sin. Absolutely mind-blowing!

Imagine being there in that moment where Jesus breathed on His disciples as He gave them this authority to forgive. One minute they are powerless men, completely unable to affect the condition of humanity, and in the next, they contain within themselves the promise of supreme authority to release people from the one problem that has held man imprisoned for thousands of years!

Jesus, in His extravagance, not only gave us the ability to forgive, He also gave us the ability to choose to forgive! In effect, He gave us a sovereignty in which He expects us to operate. I realise that when I say this some will automatically assume I am placing man equal, or above, God. Let me put you at ease now: I am definitely not going to go there. God is a sovereign God. But just as

177

a king here on earth in his own country has a measure of sovereignty, so too, our Father in heaven has entrusted to us a measure of sovereignty—a sovereignty of choice.

In that moment when Jesus breathed on man, He restored the partnership that God formed with man in the garden of Eden in the very beginning. It was a partnership where God willingly chose to give us a place of influence in the way things play out. That is one scary thought! It would be irresponsible for us then, to let sin and sickness run rampant and then point the finger at God as if it is His fault. And yet we still do! He commissioned us to forgive those who sin against us—freeing people from the debt that sin creates. It is wrong of us to expect God to do something He has asked us to do.

In the same way, He told us to heal the sick and gave us full ability to do so through the power of the resurrection. We have power to forgive and power to heal the sick. So many people place the existence of sickness upon the sovereignty of God, when in reality, it is in the jurisdiction of our God-given authority and "sovereignty" where infirmities have been allowed to remain.

God gave Adam charge over the garden in the beginning. When weeds grew, was it God's fault or Adam's? Perhaps some would say, "The weeds are there, so it must be God's will for them to grow." Then when they grow so big that they take over the garden, we point the finger at God and say, "Why did You let these weeds grow?" That is simply irresponsible; it was not God who let the weeds grow. We were the ones who did not follow through on the delegated authority God gave us.

If we are going to play the "blame" game when it comes to this issue of healing, then we have to be willing to accept the responsibility and position God has blessed us with.

178

Just because something has happened does not automatically mean it is the will of God for that thing to happen. There is plenty that happens in this world that God never allowed or wanted to happen. To start with, it definitely was not His will for Adam to eat the fruit from the tree of knowledge of good and evil, and yet, Adam ate it. He specifically had told Adam, "Do not eat from that tree!" Yet Adam and Eve went and did it anyway. Does that mean it became God's will for Adam to eat that fruit? No! It simply establishes the fact that man exercised a God-given free will.

Oftentimes the mindset that uses God's sovereignty to give place to sickness is rooted in a belief that God is in full control. It was a revelation to me that all authority and all control are two very different things. Yes, God has all authority, but He relegated control on earth to man. How is it God's will that none should perish and yet people choose to deny Him and perish every day? If God was in control of man's will this would not be! My father-in-law says it well: "I am in control of my house. I can choose what I want to do with my house: I can choose to sell it or I can choose to keep it. But that does not mean I am in control of the people in my house."

In the beginning, God gave Adam and Eve charge over the earth. He placed it in their control. When they chose to sin, they handed their God-given control and their authority over to the devil.

Jesus came and restored us to back to life and reinstated our original mandate: to take dominion of the earth. It was never God's desire to take back control given to man in the garden. Rather, by Jesus' death and resurrection He took back the authority we had given to satan at the fall. We, then, became His body on the earth exercising and activating His authority in power.

179

Jesus fully restored our ability to govern the earth again. We have been given these governing powers as part of our inheritance, not to lord control over each other, but to love each other, rule over the enemy, and exercise control over creation.

People wonder why there are natural disasters and widespread catastrophes in the world today. Because of a lack of understanding these events often get explained away as "God's will." The only reason events like these are allowed to happen is because sin is still present in the world. Even though the bondage of sin has been defeated, it is still very much present through the thoughts and actions of people who choose to sin. This sin gives ground for the enemy to operate and to do what he does best: steal, kill, and destroy.

The results of sin cause creation to react and respond in unnatural ways. God's creation was never designed to be exposed to sin and its effects. If there was no sin on the earth, satan would have no territory in which to operate. He would just be a powerless lizard in a tree and all of creation would be at peace. Why else do you think the Scripture says that creation is anxiously awaiting for the sons of God to be revealed?[8] It is our commission and awesome privilege to partner with God in this ministry of reconciliation: the great reunion of the world and all of creation back to the Father.

I love the way The Message puts it:

> *You put us in charge of Your handcrafted world,*
> *repeated to us Your Genesis-charge.*
>
> Psalms 8:6, MSG

The New English Translation puts it like this:

> *You appoint them to rule over Your creation; You*

have placed everything under their authority.

The writer of Hebrews says it like this:

> *You have crowned him* [man] *with glory and honour, and have appointed him over the works of Your hands; You have put all things in subjection under his feet. For in subjecting all things to him, He left nothing that is not subject to him.*

2:7-8

The NET Bible says it like this:

> *"You put all things under his* [mans'] *control." For when he put all things under his control, he left nothing outside of his control.*

The word for "subjection" or "control" in this passage from Hebrews literally means, "to subordinate; to be under obedience." To be subordinate means to be lower in rank and to be under the authority and control of another. We have been given the ability to control by the Owner of our planet. We can see that the real reason creation can be out of control is because we, who are ruling, have not taken the proper responsibility and managed our relegated control well. God gave us this control and He desires that we will rule and reign in the full power of His Spirit.

Whenever there is chaos and disorder in creation, whether it be in the world around us or in our physical bodies, He has given us authority and control over it.

We live in an extremely exciting time. Believers all over the globe are beginning to walk in an awareness that they have been given authority over all the works of the enemy and over every situation that arises here on earth. With this heightened awareness, we, as a body are learning to take more and more responsibility recognizing we have heaven's answer to every problem we encounter. As we do, the Lord will begin to entrust His children with the fullness of His power to outwork the fullness of His kingdom here on earth.

We are starting to see the fullness of His glory washing over the earth, just as He intended it to be from the beginning! It might only be a cloud the size of a man's hand on the distant horizon, but it won't be long until it will be a mighty downpour of God's glory that floods the earth! May we be known in heaven as those who walk in the fullness of the Kingdom that has been given to us!

The prophet Daniel saw in a vision a time where the saints would take possession of the Kingdom and he described what he saw.

> *Then the **sovereignty**, the **dominion** and the greatness of all the kingdoms under the whole heaven **will be given to the people of the saints of the Highest One**; His kingdom will be an everlasting kingdom, and all the dominions will serve and obey Him.*
>
> Daniel 7:27, emphasis added

Jesus' death and resurrection was the establishment of His everlasting Kingdom on the earth. He came, and announced:

> *The time is fulfilled, and the kingdom of God is at hand.*
>
> Mark 1:15

He also said:

The kingdom of God is in your midst [or within you].

Luke 17:21

This truly is the age of the possession of God's kingdom! He destroyed death and released the sovereignty, dominion, and greatness of all the kingdoms under heaven to us. That is why He can expect us to disciple nations.[9] He has put all things in subjection to His kingdom and He has put His kingdom within us. May we be those who realise the full responsibility of the position and authority He has given us! May we faithfully steward the Kingdom within us to see the kingdoms of this world become the kingdoms of our God!

Case 3: The Pool of Bethesda

It seems that although many people accept God's will to heal, they still believe that it is His will to heal some, but not others.

Biblical accounts, like the pool of Bethesda where Jesus healed only one man but not everyone at the pool, are often used to support this theology. The real problem with this view is that it is inconsistent with many other Scriptures where Jesus "healed all." When He died on the cross, He actually paid with His own blood for all to be healed.

We know that Jesus Himself is the perfect representation of the Father and His perfect will. As we see Jesus, we get a perfectly clear and transparent view straight into the depths of the heart of the Father for His people.

With this, it is important to look at Jesus' ministry of healing, knowing He perfectly represented the Father's heart. We see numerous times where Jesus healed "all"

183

who came to Him. Not once do we ever read of Him turning away a person who came to Him needing healing. The only person that seemed like Jesus was turning away was the Syrophoenician woman. Some think Jesus tried to send her away. He actually did not. He simply remained silent while His disciples were suggesting that He send her away because she would not stop shouting![10] Her insistence was annoying them! Although Jesus gave some crazy answers to the woman's cry for help, He absolutely did not reject her request for healing nor did He send her away. In this amazing exchange when it seemed like Jesus and this woman are speaking to each other in their own language, He did not shut the door to her, but rather, gave her two opportunities. These two opportunities are still offered to us in most situations today: take offence, or jump over the offence and take what you need. Oftentimes, to get what we need requires we must leave our intellectual offences at the door and come to Him with our whole heart trusting. About Jesus, Bill Johnson puts it best when he says:

He will offend the mind to reveal the heart.

Jesus never sent anyone away who came to Him. That is important for us to remember as we consider God's desire to heal.

The blind man, Bartimaeus, is another amazing example of God's beautiful heart to hear and to heal. Jesus was not heading towards the blind man to heal him; He was simply walking his direction intending to pass on by him. But Bartimaeus decided he was not going to let this opportunity pass him by.

Hearing the commotion of the crowd around Jesus, he began to shout, "Jesus! Jesus! Have mercy on me!" Here again, it was not Jesus who told him to be quiet. It was the people! But when Jesus heard him shouting, He responded completely opposite to the crowds!

"Call him here!" Jesus shouted out in response. Everyone in the crowd was hushing the blind man, "Shut up! Go away!" The fact is, a blind person of the first century was considered cursed and of no worth or value.

But the compassion of Jesus caused Him to hear this man's desperate pleas above the noise of the great crowd of people.

"Call him here!" He instructed the people near to the blind man.

So, too, the Syrophoenician woman was desperately pleading on behalf of her daughter. And the result of her encounter with Jesus is that her daughter was healed.

Jesus healed all who came to Him. *All.* He never sent anyone away. Even the woman with the 12-year bleeding condition, pushing her way through the crowd, got what she needed. She took her complete healing without Jesus even anticipating it!

All who came to Jesus received what they asked for.

My conviction with those at the pool of Bethesda is this: everyone at the pool that day had the same opportunity to be healed as blind Bartimaeus did on the road to Jericho; but we do not read about any of them crying out to Jesus. Jesus was sent by the Father to heal that disabled man right in the middle of all those other needy people. This was not an act of exclusivity, but rather, a display of God's heart toward everyone at that pool.

Yet, like so many others who were eyewitnesses to Jesus' earthly life, those who were not healed that day missed what God was saying to them. His heart was to heal them, and He was putting His Son right in the middle of them so they had front-row access to the Son of God Himself. This was not an act of favouritism, but rather, an open invitation! Yet the others who needed healing did not lift their voice and call to Him or reach out and grab hold of His robe; they made no attempt to come to Him in any way.

The atmosphere in that place is probably best summed up in the disabled man's answer to Jesus questioning him. Jesus asked the man, "Do want to get well?" You know when Jesus asks someone who has been sick for thirty-eight years if they want to get well, there is bound to be a good reason. We see the man's heart revealed by his answer. He had the opportunity to simply say, "Yes!" But instead, he gives an excuse as to why he is still disabled. Whenever we give an excuse for sickness to stay, we are releasing our personal permission for it to remain.

Jesus refused to respond to this man's excuse and instead, He put on display the heart and will of the Father towards him. Jesus replies in a direct way and says, "Get up, pick up your pallet, and walk."

Notice that Jesus does not even pray for the man, He simply commands him to "get up!" And in this command, Jesus releases the power for the man to obey it. So it is when we release the command of heaven on the earth.

I believe the atmosphere around that pool was summed up in that man's response to Jesus' question. It was an atmosphere that created an excuse which allowed sickness to stay. I believe it is for this very reason we are not reading about countless others being healed by Jesus in that moment around the pool as well. Imagine what it would have been like had the others recognised the invitation that was given to them right then! Imagine what we would be reading had they chosen to be more like

Bartimaeus who forsook any possible excuse and called out in desperation. Instead, we see a group of people who chose to remain in an atmosphere which probably said, "I wish Jesus would have come over here and done that for me instead of going over there to that man." They simply did not realise that He was there for all who asked of Him.

I have decided I am not going to get to heaven and discover that what I desired all along was within arm's reach, but I totally missed it because of my excuses. We often tune in to the voices of powerless people who try to keep us from recklessly pursuing Jesus. If they have influence over our thinking, we can begin to form excuses to support a mindset that keeps us from running with the full measure Jesus intended for us. I have determined, and made up my mind, to run to Jesus daily, to jump into His arms, and if need be, drag myself out of the trenches of life and grab hold of the fringes of His robe. No matter what it looks like, I have this determination to come to Him and stay with Him until I get my hands on that which He has put within reach. I refuse to bow to the intellectual offences that come each and every day. I have determined to crash through every hurdle of offence with my heart running after Him. As much as it hurts and as much as it breaks me, I am not going to let the fullness that Jesus gave me on that cross escape simply because I did not reach for it.

All too often the spirit of the world tries to keep us from recklessly reaching for that which is within arms' reach. And oftentimes it is masked in human understanding and logic. I will not sacrifice the fullness of life with Jesus on the altar of humanism. It is not always easy, and it generally does not make sense, but the heart must rule the mind or we will simply go nowhere. The tree of the knowledge of good and evil can never make sense of the Tree of Life. Selah.

What Would We Do?

I often consider how the church today would have handled the man at the pool of Bethesda after hearing his excuse. I get the feeling we would have lectured him on the fact that he has no faith, making sure he understood that "this is the reason you are sick!" This too is an excuse that removes the responsibility from us and leaves him unchanged. Jesus demonstrated the Father's perfect will towards such a man. He heard the heart of a hurting child who had been suffering for thirty-eight long years. In His compassion, Jesus recognised that this man's excuses were the result of a heart in great pain that had become discouraged over the years. Jesus saw that the most effective way to deal with this man's heart problem was to simply answer him with a demonstration of love. He did not argue with him or "Bible-bash" him; He simply healed him. He showed the man love by giving him what he needed.

The healing power of God is always love in action.

Case 4: Paul's Thorn

Citing the Scripture of Paul's, "thorn in the flesh," seems to be a favourite of many that give permission to sickness. It is especially used where people have received prayer for healing numerous times but have seen no evidence of change. Please know that when I address this topic, I completely understand why people would take this view. Our own personal story brought us face-to-face with this very way of thinking and we were tempted many times to take the stance that this was just our "thorn."

For those of you who agree with what I say, I urge you not to use this as an argument with others who disagree. Remember that most people who have come to the conclusion that they have been given a "thorn in their flesh" are facing unbearable circumstances of sickness. These people do not need to hear another good argument; they need the power of God manifested in His love. Remember, above all, love.

Let us examine this passage of Paul's.

I know a man in Christ who fourteen years ago—whether in the body I do not know, or out of the body I do not know, God knows— such a man was caught up to the third heaven. And I know how such a man—whether in the body or apart from the body I do not know, God knows—was caught up into Paradise and heard inexpressible words, which a man is not permitted to speak. On behalf of such a man I will boast; but on my own behalf I will not boast, except in regard to my weaknesses. For if I do wish to boast I will not be foolish, for I will be speaking the truth; but I refrain from this, so that no one will credit me with more than he sees in me or hears from me.

Because of the surpassing greatness of the revelations, for this reason, to keep me from exalting myself, there was given me a thorn in the flesh, a messenger of Satan to torment me— to keep me from exalting myself! Concerning this I implored the Lord three times that it might leave me. And He has said to me, "My grace is sufficient for you, for power is perfected in weakness." Most gladly, therefore, I will rather boast about my weaknesses, so that the power of Christ may dwell in me. Therefore I am well content with weaknesses, with insults, with

*distresses, with persecutions, with difficulties,
for Christ's sake; for when I am weak, then I
am strong.*

2 Corinthians 12:2-10

It is assumed by many that this "thorn" of Paul's
was sickness and is something that seems to be accepted
as a given. I remember growing up with an untaught
understanding that it was sickness. I never even thought
otherwise until one day, I heard someone say, "I don't
believe this thorn was speaking of sickness." At first I
thought, "This optimistic fella is ignoring what the
Scriptures plainly say!" So I looked into it again myself
only to find that it never says that it is sickness. Like
so many others, I had simply come to that conclusion
without considering any other possibilities.

Paul's discussion of this matter actually begins in
chapter ten. He starts by addressing a question of his
authority and apostleship which continues right through
to the end of the book. The context for the whole of
chapter twelve is the authenticity and authority of Paul's
leadership and the message he brings.

It seems there were some who compared Paul to
other apostles and who even questioned his authority
because he did not look or sound like the others. They
even questioned the fact that in his letters he sounded
so bold, but in person, he spoke in a meek and a gentle
manner. Paul responds by taking the very thing they
believe discredits him—his "weakness"—and declares
this to be his greatest boast of all.

In verse 10 he lists a number of things of which he
is "content . . . for Christ's sake . . ."—none are sickness.

*Therefore I am well content with weaknesses,
with insults, with distresses, with persecutions,*

with difficulties, for Christ's sake; for when I am weak, then I am strong.

Some translations have used the word "infirmities" instead of "weakness." The context for this passage found in the last line where Paul writes:

For when I am weak, then I am strong.

For this reason I believe "weakness" is the correct interpretation given the context of these four verses.[11]

It is important to consider what Paul was *not* saying: "When I am sick, then I am strong." His point was that he chose to be okay with persecutions; he chose not to fight back—not because of a lack of authority, but rather, in weakness, he knew Christ would shine as his strength. He was not giving them a theology that allowed for sickness to remain. The astounding healings that came through the life of Paul were proof. His point in this verse was to boast about the source of his strength—giving glory to the God of all grace—showing his audience that it was in fact, the weakness they were offended by that was the very part of him that the Father moved through.

It is an incorrect assumption to believe Paul's "thorn" was sickness and then build theology around it.

Personally I believe that this "thorn" Paul spoke of was the severe persecution he faced so frequently. Imagine if every time you spoke somewhere, you were beaten up, insulted, spat on, thrown out, or stoned. That is definitely a thorn I would be asking the Lord to remove!

There was given me a thorn in the flesh, a messenger from Satan to torment me—to keep me from exalting myself.

v. 7

191

The word "torment" literally means, "beat." A messenger was sent from satan to beat him. In the previous chapter Paul was just talking about the severity of the persecution he had faced for the sake of the gospel. He lists all the afflictions he had encountered thus far and even adds that when someone else is experiencing weakness, or is in sin, he feels it![12]

After outlining all of this intense pressure and persecution he states:

> *If I have to boast, I will boast of what pertains to my weakness.*
>
> v. 30

The Message puts it like this:

> *If I have to "brag" about myself, I'll brag about the humiliations that make me like Jesus.*

Paul's context of "weakness" is that which makes him like Jesus. Sickness was not one of those things. I believe the constant humiliations Paul faced—beaten, whipped, stoned, shipwrecked, starved, betrayed—were the humiliations, or the "weakness" Paul was referring to.

Look at what Paul says immediately after he mentioned the visions and revelations he had experienced.

> *If I had a mind to brag a little, I could probably do it without looking ridiculous, and I'd still be speaking plain truth all the way. But I'll spare you. I don't want anyone imagining me as anything other than the fool you'd encounter if you saw me on the street or heard me talk.*
>
> 12:6, MSG

Paul thoroughly addresses the challenge that was being brought against his apostleship from the Corinthian Church.[13] People were struggling to see how Paul could hold such a position of authority when he did not look or sound like the other apostles. Looking at 2 Corinthians 11:6 we get a profile of their description of Paul:

- He was unskilled in speech,

- He worked for his own wages,

- He was humble, and

- He did not demand financial retribution for his ministry as others did.

Not much has changed today. If we saw a ministry leader working for his own meals, uncharismatic in preaching style and poor in speech, we would probably question their qualification and authority as a leader. On top of that, if they were beaten up constantly, cast out of cities, stoned, betrayed, and generally abused everywhere they preached, we might conclude that perhaps they were not called to the ministry, and might even question if they had unresolved sin in their life!

But Paul challenges this mindset, not by pumping himself up by playing their game of "Who's had the biggest revelation?" but by boasting in what they saw as weakness. Paul uses the very things that the Corinthians felt disqualified him as the evidence of his authority to be an apostle. In their culture, and ours, it was a humiliating thing to be beaten publicly; but Paul considered such a thing worthy of boasting. It was in this context that he says:

> *Because of the surpassing greatness of the revelations, for this reason, to keep me from*

exalting myself, there was given me a thorn in
the flesh, a messenger from Satan to beat me,
to keep me from exalting myself! Concerning
this I implored the Lord three times that it might
leave me.

vs. 7-8

This fulfills what Jesus said to Ananias concerning Paul:

For I [Jesus] will show him [Paul] how much he
must suffer for My names' sake.

Acts 9:16

When we consider the context of chapters 10 through 12 in 2 Corinthians, I believe it is clear to see that Paul is referring to the persecutions he continually faced when he mentions the "thorn" in his flesh.

It is important to note that Paul never gave an excuse that allowed for sickness to stay in a person who needed healing. This is evident in the "extraordinary miracles"[14] done through Paul's ministry.

Case 5: What About Job?

In regard to suffering, the story of Job and his life of severe trials, is yet another contentious topic among many believers, and for good reason. At first glance, this book seems like the story of a pawn used in a dispute between God and satan over some bragging rights.

The first thing we need to understand in order to correctly interpret this story is that God never responds to the devil. If He did, that would place the devil in control. But the devil is never in control; he merely casts the illusion that he is in control in order to initiate fear. However, that illusion obviously does not work on God.

194

This unique story starts out with the "sons of God" coming and presenting themselves before Him:

> *Now there was a day when the sons of God came to present themselves before the LORD, and Satan also came among them.*

Job 1:6

We often read this opening chapter in a way that makes God out to be an insecure Being who has to prove Himself against the taunts of satan. We know this is far from true, and yet we can often trace our perception of God's overall authority and rule back to this lie.

We know God cannot be manipulated or controlled by the devil. That being the case, what really happened in this strange encounter of which Job is unknowingly at the centre?

As well as understanding that God does not respond to the devil, we also need to appreciate the historical period of this encounter. If we do not, we run the risk of creating a powerless theology that Jesus never once taught. Perhaps the single most important truth we need to acknowledge in this story is that it occurred prior to the cross. This is central. Before Jesus came to earth, the devil had legal rights that entitled him to the authority we handed over to him in the garden.

Although Job was blameless and upright, he was not righteous. Paul quotes the psalmist about the condition of man before Christ came:

> *There is none righteous, not even one.*

Romans 3:10

Another indicator of the time period that this encounter took place is the fact that God refers to Job as

His "servant," indicating this was under the Old Covenant:

Have you considered My servant Job?

Job 1:8

If this conversation took place under the New Covenant, Job would have been called "son." In the time of the Old Covenant, a servant meant "slave."

Job's life was lived in the pre-cross period. That means, the sins of men had not yet been covered by the blood of Christ and the human race was enslaved in bondage to the devil. This gave the devil legal right to exercise his earthly authority over Job. What amazes me about this story is that even though the devil had legal right over the affairs of man, God still "broke the rules" and placed a hedge of protection around Job so that he would be greatly blessed and prosper exceedingly. This demonstrates the heart of God our Father in His great desire to love and protect us—even while the devil exercised his legal right over man because of sin.

Further on we read:

Then Satan answered the LORD, "Does Job fear God for nothing? Have You not made a hedge about him and his house and all that he has, on every side?"

vs. 9-10

The devil was basically saying, "Job has not had a bad day in his life, and you have made him untouchable on every side—even to me!" It was God's amazing grace that kept Job healthy, strong, and prosperous in an age where the devil actively exercised his rights over the affairs of man. When we look at this story in the context of history, we do not see a God who is trying to prove Himself to the devil. Instead we see God releasing His abundant grace that protects a sinner and places an impenetrable boundary around him, making him untouchable by the enemy.

The question still remains, "Why did God give the devil access to Job?" Simply put, the devil had legal right to Job because of sin. When the devil came before God that day, he put a demand on what legally belonged to him because our sin had given it to him.

We need to remember that the moment God gave us authority on earth, He invited us into a place where our decisions hold weight. We suddenly had the ability to make decisions that affected the heart of God! God made Himself vulnerable to us. Not in a way where we can manipulate Him or cause Him to change who He is, but rather in a way where He experiences both the joy and the heartache of our decisions. Deep relationship requires vulnerability and trust. It requires the kind of openness that says to another person, "You have the ability to bless or hurt my heart. I trust you to protect and value it." This depth of relationship is when two hearts are joined in such a way where if either one of them makes a decision, the other experiences the full weight of it.

When God gave us authority on earth, He did not do so casually. He gave it to us in trust. He made Himself vulnerable to us. We see the effects of this here in Job's story. The devil came and demanded access to someone's life that he had been handed legal access to because of that broken relationship from the time of the garden. I cannot imagine how much that must have broken God's heart to have to lift the hedge of protection around Job. He did not do it in response to the devil, but to honour man's choice in the garden.

This discussion between the devil and God was not

a matter of God proving Himself through Job. His final decision was a result that began in the garden of Eden and was still in effect. The devil was given access to man by his own God-given free will choice. Now all these years later he was doing his best again to rob God of the part of creation that He had given His heart to—man.

Some people say, "But isn't God sovereign? Couldn't He just have chosen not to lift that hedge of protection?" That is exactly the type of vulnerability that came with the relationship God shared with man in that garden. Yes, God is sovereign; that is why He had the hedge of protection there in the first place. But in His sovereignty He gave us authority, and that authority is real and holds weight. And even though it breaks God's heart, He will still honour the choices we choose to make.

The devil also knew the validity of man's authority. He understood the rights he had been handed. We see evidence of this in satan's extreme efforts to tempt Jesus into worshipping him.

> *And the devil said to Him, "I will give You all this domain and its glory; **for it has been handed over to me, and I give it to whomever I wish.** Therefore if You worship before me, it shall all be Yours."*
>
> Luke 4:6-7, emphasis added

Notice Jesus did not reply, "Liar! That is not yours to give." Jesus knew it was the devil's to give, but He was not willing to compromise His connection with the Father in order to get it. The devil always offers through compromise and disobedience what God has already promised to us through relationship. It was the same in the garden with Adam and Eve, it was the same with Jesus in the wilderness, and his tactics are the same with us today.

About healing, I hear this said a lot, "But, what about Job?" What they are saying is, "Doesn't God allow sickness to prove a point?"

My usual response to the question of "What about Job?" is "What about Jesus?" I believe many people have developed a flawed view of God simply because they read Job without understanding that it is pre-blood, pre-cross, and pre-redemption.

We must understand that the account of Job took place in a different age. The blood of Jesus changed everything! If it was not for Jesus, the devil would have the same legal access to every single one of us today. But in Christ, we have been bought and reborn. We have been made righteous! Unlike Job we are no longer slaves; we are sons and daughters of God through Christ. If we neglect the fact of the blood, as we review Job's story, we are leaving out the single most important event in all of history! The blood of Jesus is the pivot point of human history, marking the moment when the authority the devil had been given was recovered and restored back to man through our new positional relationship in Christ.

The only way the devil gains the type of legal access that he had in Job is through sin. You have received forgiveness in Christ and are now a new creation through Him. Where, then, is the devil's access point into your life? Nowhere! You are no longer a sinner; you are identified as a saint! Not only has God forgiven your past, He has made you completely new! You no longer have a sin nature! When we remain in Him, we position ourselves in alignment with Jesus where the devil has nothing in us.[15]

It is a dangerous thing to develop an interpretation of the New Covenant from the Old Covenant whilst discounting the blood of Jesus. In doing so, we create a

THE ART OF HEALING

"Christ-less" theology—a belief system that overlooks the very person our life is founded upon. To look into the Old Covenant without looking through the lens of the blood of Christ will only cause us to develop a belief system that neglects the most powerful substance in human existence: the blood of Jesus!

Remember, pre-cross, there was no payment for sin or sickness; post-cross, there is complete payment for both sin and sickness. Praise God!

One of my favourite insights that is brought to light through the book of Job is our position as believers. As we see in the opening chapter, satan came with the sons of God before God. How could he do this? Simple. He had been given legitimate authority from those whom God intended to be sons. When? In the garden when man fell and we handed to him all the authority we had. Now in the post-cross age, satan has been completely stripped of that authority. We know this because Jesus says, "All authority has been given to Me."[16] If Jesus has all, then somebody has none. That somebody is the devil. There is absolutely none left over for him to exercise. Jesus has it all!

In Christ, we have been given back the authority we lost, meaning, we have also been given back the position we once held because our authority only comes from our position of relationship with the Father. The devil used to be able to come before the Lord and accuse us like he did to Job. Now because he has been stripped of the authority we handed him, he is no longer able to do that.

Jesus said He saw satan fall like lightning from heaven.[17] When did He see this happen? It was as the disciples moved in the power of Jesus performing miracles and setting people free. It was as man took back the authority that was rightfully theirs in Christ.

The devil is still very much the accuser of the brethren, but he has no legal right or authority. We, on the other hand, have been given back the authority and position we originally held. In Christ, we are able to present ourselves before the Father. In Christ, we are able to decree and establish things in the Spirit and in the natural. The place the devil once held—to walk before the presence of God—has been handed back to us! Paul confirms this:

> *But God, being rich in mercy, because of His great love with which He loved us, even when we were dead in our transgressions, made us alive together with Christ* [by grace you have been saved], *and raised us up with Him, and seated us with Him **in the heavenly places** in Christ Jesus.*
>
> Ephesians 2:4-6, emphasis added[18]

Included in the fullness of this beautiful restoration is the ability to come boldly before the throne of our Father.[19] This is a privilege we held in the beginning but lost for thousands of years. Then in a glorious display of love and grace, we were given again this unparalleled position of undeserved favour to walk before the all-pure, all-powerful, Almighty Creator Himself. The amazing thing is that we did not obtain this position by earning it back through works. No, we have this unique position in creation because He chose for us to have it. God the Father so desires that we would walk with Him, talk with Him, live with Him, and laugh with Him.

This is the relationship He has longed for since the garden.

End Notes

1. 1 Cor. 6:19.
2. See Mark 5.
3. See Matt. 8:5-13.
4. Rom. 5:8.
5. See John 20:23.
6. See Acts 7:54-60.
7. See Mark 16:17-18.
8. See Rom. 8:19.
9. See Matt. 28:19.
10. See Matt. 15.23.
11. See 2 Cor. 12:7-10.
12. See 2 Cor. 11:29.
13. See 2 Cor. 10 through 12.
14. See Acts 19:11.
15. See John 14:30.
16. Ibid.
17. See Luke 10:18.
18. Author's notes.
19. See Heb. 4:16.

ASSIGNMENT 6

Healing on Main Street

This time we are going to go for a walk down one of the main streets in your town or city at a time when there are a number of other people around. As you walk, ask the Lord to show you someone who has a need of healing. As you are walking down the street, speak to whomever it is that stands out to you.

Approach the person and ask them if they have a need of healing. You can say something like this:

> *Hi there. I am learning about hearing God's voice and about how He loves to heal people. And as I was walking, I felt to ask you if you have any pain in your body that you need God to heal?*

If the person says, "No," gently ask them again.

> *Are you sure you don't have a sore back or neck or something?*

Oftentimes people are caught off guard and don't know how to respond to such a request so they initially respond with, "No." But I have found that when I ask them again, even several times, they finally reply, "Oh yea, I have had pain in my back for a while now."

As you're talking to them, stay aware of the Holy Spirit and listen to any thoughts that pop into your mind as it is most often Him speaking. You might have a thought of a particular condition or a body part that needs healing.

When you get this thought from the Holy Spirit, ask the person:

❖ *"Do you have pain in your _____?" or*

❖ *"Do you suffer from _____?" and mention what the Holy Spirit brought to mind.*

If they acknowledge they have a need of healing, ask permission to place your hand on their shoulder and pray for them. (If it's appropriate, and you feel to, place your hand on the specific area that needs healing.)

As you pray for them, bind the pain or the condition, release healing and the love of God, and then ask the person to test it out.

From there, you know what to do. If the pain remains, pray again. If it gets better, thank the Lord for what He is doing and ask Him for more.

❖ *If the person continues to say they have no pain or ill condition in their body after you have asked them, thank them for their time and continue on down the road. Then ask the Lord for another target to release His love towards!*

Releasing the Kingdom is as easy as walking down the street!

I feel overcome
With hurt and pain
The brokenness
It's overwhelming
I'm crying out,
"Lord, deliver me!"
Still I know
You are God
And God alone
Your goodness
Has been clearly shown
I know You have revealed
Yourself to me

"Help Me Jesus"
by Josh Klinkenberg

CHAPTER 11

The Elijah

Story

It was the 8th of July 2008, a Tuesday morning. My wife started to feel the slight cramps of labor coming on early that morning. Like any first-time Dad I had absolutely no idea what was going on or what was about to happen. I was working as a builder with my brother-in-law at that time and decided to head to work anyway that morning. I asked Amberley to call me if I needed to return home since we were working just under an hour away. As I said, I had no idea what was coming!

We had been at work all of five minutes when I got the call from my wife letting me know that the contractions were getting stronger and stronger. Needless to say, I raced all the way back home.

My wife and I made our way to the birthing clinic and we set ourselves up in one of the rooms. We were the only family in there that day so it was nice to have the private space and a peaceful atmosphere. Amberley, myself and our midwife were sitting around listening to worship music waiting for the baby to kick-start the birthing process. There was such a sweet presence in that room that I turned to my wife and said, "The last time I felt this kind of presence was when we were at a Heidi and Rolland Baker conference." It was thick!

MacGyver, Is That You?

I needed to go to the bathroom, so I went and found it just down the hall, off to the side and out of the way. I headed into the small men's room with a single toilet and basin in it, shutting the door behind me.

It was a good opportunity to take a moment before heading back to the labor room just to steady my nerves in preparation for the most significant event in any family's life, welcoming a new baby into the world. Ready to return, I reached for the door handle to open it, but it was locked! I jiggled it back and forth thinking maybe it was just stiff. But I discovered quickly that it was definitely locked and refused to budge.

I felt panic begin to rise within me. In that moment I started to wonder if I would be the guy who missed his son's birth because he was locked inside the toilet! Needless to say, I did not want to be that guy.

I suddenly remembered the clinics admission's clerk mentioning that they had remodelled the clinic and that the painters had just been in. That is when I realised they had put the door handle on the wrong way and it was locked from the outside.

I looked out the window and quickly measured the fall to the ground below. I thought, *I reckon I could make that.* It was only about a one-story drop onto a sharp, sloping grassy hill. Then I thought, *I don't wanna be the guy who had a broken leg and was rushed to the Emergency Room while his wife is in labor with his first child . . .* So I decided I needed to try something else first.

Then I got the idea about trying to kick the door open. I did not really want to have to pay for the damage of the door, though retelling the story would sound pretty heroic. So I positioned myself with my arms against the back wall of the toilet room and lifted my foot, partially excited about having a legitimate excuse to kick down a door! Before I got the chance to fulfill one of my childhood dreams, I was standing there with my leg-cocked ready to go, when my eye caught something. I saw that the door opened towards me. I was still tempted to give it a go, but I knew deep down inside, that instead of looking like a hero, I would be the guy who got stuck in the toilet whilst trying to kick the door in the wrong way! I did not want to be that guy either. So that option was ruled out.

Then I had this strange thought: *Can I pick the lock?* I had never picked locks before but I used to watch MacGyver, so I figured that must count for something! I looked at the lock and knew I would need a long, narrow object if this plan was going to work. Then it hit me, *my belt!* I was wearing my trusty black, leather belt that had the standard metal belt buckle mechanism which I figured would probably work. My hero, MacGyver, would have had his trusty Swiss Army knife on him that would have made this challenge all too easy. I pulled the belt from around my waist and began to manoeuvre the little metal pin into place. All the while I was silently praying, "Please God, let this work! I do not want to miss my son's birth."

209

For some reason, I had resolved in my mind the fact that if I did not make it out of there, they would never know where I was! It makes me laugh now that the thought that scared me most was that my wife would not know where I was or what happened to me. I felt like I would be lost, never to be heard from again! I would be the guy living out my days alone . . . in the men's room . . . in a toilet stall. Dramatic, I know! I had forgotten that the birthing clinic was not all that big, and before long, they would probably send someone to find out where I was. To me, however, this moment was a matter of life and death!

I was working the pin of my belt around in that door, hoping and praying that something would give. In the back of my mind I was starting to think about the jump out the window again. *Surely it could not be that bad,* I thought. I even considered the fact that if I broke my leg, I probably would not have to head to hospital straight away. I figured it would be sore but I could probably hold out for my son's birth and then head to hospital afterwards. Isn't it funny how fear makes you think in a way that makes no sense at all?

Click. I heard a noise that sounded like a thousand angels singing praises to the King! It was the sound of freedom . . . the sound of deliverance . . . the sound of the toilet stall door opening!

I had done it! The door lock popped open! *Yes!* I turned the door handle and felt such a wave of relief as the door opened. I took a few breaths, composed myself, and got to a place where I felt like I could "play it cool" and walk back into the room where my wife was. I was able to comfort her with the knowledge that she was married to someone with the heroic skills of MacGyver. It is funny how as soon as I left the men's room, somehow I could not remember being the panicked little boy, only that I was more like a Hollywood hero.

A Storm Like No Other

Finally the moment came where our son was ready to be born. With one final push he came out right into my hands. I had never experienced anything like it!

Our midwife wrapped Elijah in a towel and handed him to my wife. We were in awe of this beautiful boy who had just entered our lives. Because this was our first child we had no idea that he was supposed to be crying. We were just in awe . . . adoring him—so in love with our firstborn son.

The midwife surprised me as she suddenly began to rough him up a little, wiping his face with a towel. I shrugged it off as normal. Calmly she took Elijah over to the medical baby bed and attempted to make him cough to help him take his first breath. That was about the time she turned to me with a look of fierce determination and commanded in a grave tone, "Pray!"

Suddenly, the reality of the situation hit us like a sledgehammer to the gut. *Were we going to lose our baby boy before we even got to meet him? What was going on?* My mind was invaded with a whirlwind of thoughts. A half dozen nurses and medical staff seemed to materialise out of thin air. The room was now filled with nurses rushing here and there as my wife lay on the birthing bed in shock. The joy of the first moments of our son's birth now vanished. My wife looked as if she were dead inside as an emotional paralysis began to set in. I saw the nurses trying to make the newborn bed work with its built-in heater, which for some reason was not turning on. I found a gap in the nurses that surrounded my son and saw a fragile little baby lying there fighting for his life. I reached out my hand and placed it on him and as soon as I did, he seemed to acknowledge me by looking directly at me and making a noise.

Before I knew it, the emergency team from the hospital had shown up and put Elijah on life support. We were rushed to an ambulance and were on our way to the hospital—about to begin a journey no one could have warned us about.

When we arrived, my wife was rushed up to the women's ward. They took my son to the Newborn Intensive Care Unit (NICU). I went to make sure my wife was okay. She was still in shock and seemed numb to what was going on around her. Her dream of having a baby and holding the son that she had been carrying for 9-months had just been ripped away. She had emotionally shut down in an effort to survive.

We were not designed to be exposed to this kind of trauma. God did not make us in a way where it is natural to deal with this kind overwhelming pain. God's intention is always perfect peace and love. His intention was the garden. That all changed, however, when man opened the door to the devil. The earth was not created to withstand the damaging effects of sin because it was never meant to be exposed to it in the first place.

I had to leave my wife in the hospital room while I went down to the NICU to check on our newborn son. I walked in to see him attached to several machines, with tubes coming out of every part of his body and with wires running in every direction. They were keeping him on ice to reduce any brain swelling that might occur as a result of being starved of oxygen over an extended period of time.

The doctors came in that night and gave me a brief run down on what they knew thus far, which was pretty much nothing. By now it was close to one A.M. and both the doctors and medical staff, as well as my family, were urging me to go home and sleep. I walked down to my car alone.

This is not the way it was supposed to be, I thought. *I went to the clinic with my wife this morning and we were supposed to leave with our son. Now I am leaving alone.* I had to leave my wife alone in a hospital room with several other patients. My son was hooked up to more machines than I knew existed for a baby his size in a room full of strangers. *And here I am, going home . . . alone.*

I got into my car, put the key into the ignition and attempted to turn it. It would not move. I felt a wave of shock and emotion hit me. It was like I had stepped out into the path of a bus. The intensity of it had paralysed me. I could not see for the blinding tears but neither could I control the sobbing. The pain of what just happened started to set in. The thought of my baby boy being left all alone up there in a hospital, not knowing what was going on was just to much for me to bear. I never knew it was possible to love someone you did not even know so deeply. Selah.

Our midwife came to visit the next day and said she went back to test the baby bed and write a report for it to be fixed as they could not get the heater working while we were there. She went into the room and tried it one last time only to find everything worked perfectly. We found out from the doctors later that week that if the heater had have turned on, the brain swelling in our son would have most likely been a lot more severe.

Death, Where is Your Sting?

I sat back down with a cup of instant coffee that had become the taste of comfort to me over the past month. The styrofoam cups were clumsy at first, and always threatened to jump right out of my hand onto the floor of the NICU. What started as a love-hate relationship with these stubborn little cups had grown into a close friendship over the last number of weeks. The barstool I had claimed for the day was awkwardly high, even for me at 6'2". It too was incredibly uncomfortable at first, but over the last few weeks, my body had somehow adjusted to the daily use of this hard, unforgiving barstool. It allowed me to sit at a height where I could see over the side of Elijah's cot. He was lying less that 12-inches from me.

I had just settled back into my spot in the corner of the room after a short break from the daily routine of sitting at my son's bedside. Usually there were as many as six other little ones in the same room, but today, it was much quieter than normal. There were only two other babies in Elijah's room and I was enjoying the peace.

Apart from the occasional checkup from a nurse, the room was empty of adult presence—just me, and my book, tucked away in the corner. I was reading about one of my heroes, Smith Wigglesworth. I found that while the storm was raging all around me, one of the best things to do was to keep my eyes on the awesome power of God. I had seen firsthand how easily we, as human beings, can forget the goodness of God, and I for one did not want to travel any further down that road. So I read books of testimonies of what God had done in years past. My son was sleeping soundly, which allowed me to take a moment to chew through some more stories and feed my soul on the faithfulness of our Father.

I had only been reading a short while when I began to see something. My head was down, looking at the book, and yet I could see the whole room as if I was perched up in the corner behind me where the ceiling and walls meet. I could see Elijah right there in front of me, and I could see the other two babies—one on the left of my son about 3-meters away, and the other straight ahead about 5-meters away on the other side of the room.

As I continued to look I saw what looked like a dark fog come in through the wall of the room onto the other two babies. It rested on them for a while and then I saw it "look" at my son. It had no face or features and yet I could tell it was looking for prey. It began to move towards my son and I could almost see a hand trying to reach out from the darkness grabbing at my boy. Then I saw light begin to shine. It was coming from Elijah. It began to shine brighter and brighter until I could not see my son anymore. Then is started to grow. As it grew the darkness retreated, almost nervously, like it had awakened an age-old foe.

Suddenly I was sitting back in my chair looking at my book. Unlike some visions that need interpretation, I instantly knew what all this meant. I did not know how and I did not care. All I knew was that I had to rebuke the spirit of death and command life and light over my son. And just as death was trying to come in through these other babies to attack my son, so life would come in through my son and impact these other babies.

I whispered my prayer and conversation with the Father for the next 15 to 20 minutes. It was nothing dramatic and definitely did not seem like anything all that significant, but the Lord was about to show me the reality of what was really going on in that moment. After I had finished praying, I continued reading for a while and then headed out to lunch at the cafe across the street for an hour or so.

It is interesting to note at this point the names of the other babies with my son were Leviathan and Lucian. We could not believe that we were sitting in a room with

Elijah, Leviathan, and Lucian. It was like something out of a bad end-times movie! After talking to both sets of parents, we found out that they had backgrounds in the occult. Levi (as we called him) was named after a grandfather who was a spiritualist and Lucian was named because they liked it, and it was a derivative of Lucifer. It was awesome, really, that the Lord had placed them in with our son. Those two babies got to start their life with prophetic declarations and promises being released over them everyday for weeks! I look forward to meeting them again one day as adult men who stepped into the fullness of their God-breathed destiny as champions of heaven on the earth!

It was only three days later that I found myself standing in the hallway with Levi's mum. We were there because the doctors were doing a shift change, so they asked everyone to leave the room for 10 to 15-minutes while they updated their co-workers about their patients.

As we waited in the hallway I asked Levi's mum, "How are you doing?"

"Not bad," she replied, "but three days ago, it was a different story."

"What do you mean?" I inquired.

She explained that she had come in around lunchtime to see Levi. As she began to care for him, he suddenly turned blue and flat-lined right in her arms. The alarms were sounding and doctors rushed in from everywhere as they frantically tried to revive him. After several attempts, they were about to pronounce him dead, but one last doctor walked in and said, "Let's just try it one more time."

"So they did," Levi's mum told me, "and it was like someone just flicked on the switch. He came back to life!

He has been completely fine and doing really well ever since!"

I was shocked! This had happened only moments after I had prayed and left the room that day for lunch. It was a clear indication and confirmation of my praying over the babies.

I knew of her "spiritual" background so I knew she would understand what I had experienced.

"You would never believe what happened the other day!" I said. I went on to tell her of the vision I had seen and what the Lord had shown me.

"Jesus has amazing plans for your son's life." I continued to prophesy over Levi that God will use him in amazing ways.

Her response really surprised me. "I knew God had plans for him!" she said. "I believe it. God's gonna use him!" What I had said had somehow confirmed a deep knowing that she had unconsciously held within herself.

The full impact of seeing Levi come back to life did not hit me, however, until about four months later when I was back in our hometown. One Sunday, as I was standing in worship at our little church, the Lord clearly spoke to me and said, "You still do not get it do you?"

In that moment, I had no idea what He was referring to.

So I replied, "What do You mean?"

"You saw that baby raised from the dead," the Lord responded, "but you still do not get it!" Even with His reply, I still had no idea what He was talking about. I had no memory of that day in the hospital all those months earlier.

Then He reminded me of that day and said, "If you had not prayed, Levi would have died. That is the power of prayer."

Suddenly, I got it. Selah.

Home or Hell?

After the birth of my son we were in hospital for several months. During that time he had dozens of surgeries, tests, CAT scans, and MRIs. The enemy tried just about everything to end his life prematurely.

One afternoon, my wife and I walked into the NICU after being away for the morning. We would normally have arrived early in the morning, but on that day, we took the first half of the day to spend some much needed time together. A nurse nervously approached us after our son had awakened from his sleep.

"I need to inform you that we accidentally gave your son ten-times the charted dosage of sedative that we meant to give him." I stood there in shocked silence as I took in her words.

"We have been waiting all day for him to wake up." I realised they were fully expecting him to simply not wake up.

As we approached our son and saw him lying there wide-eyed and awake, my wife and I were gripped by God's sustaining grace, and once again we experienced His protection over our little son. He experienced no lasting affects from the overdose.

There were numerous attacks on our son's life during our time in the hospital. These were often the result of highly unusual and out of the ordinary errors by the medical staff. Many times we were informed that he was completely "brain dead." Every time we were given this particular medical evaluation, we felt a seductive pull to agree with it. But, we stood believing, refusing such finality about the mental state of our son. We refused to grant the enemy authority by believing a lie that would empower him and give him ground. We stood firm with the Healer.

Our son's mind was under severe spiritual attack during our days at the hospital. The negative reports came so frequently that it was almost an expected part of our daily hospital routine to be given a report concluding with, "severe brain-damage expected." We simply refused to believe or accept it. Every single time it was a battle we had to conquer within ourselves. And even though it made no logical sense, we always came to the point where we chose to stand with the word of our Father, the Healer.

One morning, the nurse announced to us, "There is a visitor here . . . a person who said they know your parents." At that moment a short Malaysian man came through the door and waved to us with a huge smile on his face.

We exchanged greetings and in broken English he said, "My daughter has been in a room just down the hall for a night or two. She has jaundice."

Then he walked over to Elijah's bedside where we had taken up residence the past number of weeks.

"Ah, I see your boy's name is Elijah," our new friend said.

"Yes, it is," we acknowledged.

He continued with his thick accent, "I have friend named Elijah who is genius. Your boy is gonna be genius too!"

As he spoke out these words, the force of his declaration just about knocked me over. The words themselves held such weight that they seemed to change the reality around us. I felt like I got a glimpse of what it must have been like when Jesus spoke and the group of soldiers fell back.

So when He said to them, "I am He," they drew back and fell to the ground.

John 18:6

The shift that took place in that moment standing over my son Elijah's NICU bed was an invisible one, but it felt more real than anything I had ever seen before. After our new friend had prayed, we exchanged goodbyes and he left.

From that point on, we were even more convinced of the promise of God concerning our son's mind. The enemy tried everything he could to cause us to doubt that promise. He desperately wanted us to grant him authority by agreeing with him, but we reminded ourselves daily of that moment when God had spoken. We could not deny the force of those words and the life that they carried.

Even though we seemed to be waging a continual war for life on behalf of our son, we were being sustained moment-by-moment by an unearthly peace the entire time in the hospital. It really was beyond understanding. All the while, some of the well-meaning medical staff would continually remind us, "It is only going to get worse." Many of them seemed to feel it was their obligation to make sure we were as sad and somber as possible. But, we just smiled, and continued to rest in the peace that the Lord had established deep within us. It was like the Father had placed His hand over us during this time, and because of this, we were able to bless and minister to nurses and other parents during our long stay at the hospital.

Even though there were moments of tears, and many hard decisions we had to make, the deep peace of God within us was immovable.

We heard through a friend that a year after we had left the hospital, they were still talking about "the family with a boy named Elijah" who had been such a blessing to those around them. We never once preached to them, and yet more than a year later, they still remembered the love of God in action.

We faced some real struggles when we took Elijah home. During our entire time at the hospital we felt the Father's hand over us; but at home, it felt very different. Suddenly, our inner worlds began to come crashing down. The love and joy that we had lived out in hospital was quickly swallowed up in frustration by anger and hate. We were living on virtually no sleep as our son needed constant 24-hour care—including most hours through the night.

When Elijah caught a cold, we did not even bother to attempt to sleep at night. On top of this, our son was vomiting after every feed. One of us would have to stay by his side for at least 2-hours after every single feed as he lay there trying to hold down his milk. The amount of towels we would go through during that year was unbelievable! Thank God that we had exposed concrete floors or we would have had to replace the carpet!

Because of the severe lack of sleep, the intense

pressure on both of us, and the fact that we were with each other every moment of every day, my wife and I were constantly fighting and always at each other. We had no money, no life, no space, and no joy. Things went downhill really quick.

At that time we lived in a little town called Te Aroha and we were actively involved in an awesome little church before our lives were flipped upside-down. The Holy Spirit had been moving powerfully amongst our church family. Before our son was born, we were leading worship and ministering at healing meetings regularly. I had a passion for healing and loved the opportunity to speak and pray for the sick. We were seeing some amazing things take place in that little church. The lost were getting saved, the sick were being healed, and the demon-possessed were delivered. I had seen numerous people healed physically, emotionally, and spiritually at the end of my own hands.

But now, following the birth of my son, I found I could not even bring myself to pray for God to bless someone. Every time I would try and pray for my own son I would be filled with anger. It was unthinkable to even try to pray for someone else. It would be close to two years before I would be able to pray for someone again. And that was not even a prayer that came with faith; it was just the simple act of getting the words out of my mouth!

We really loved our little church, but by this time, it had come to the point where I just could not even stay in a worship service any longer. Amberley and I would show up with Elijah. The worship would start and I would leave. I would walk out and head down the road to the dairy where I would indulge in a Kiwi Classic, a Steak and Cheese Pie, and a coke. Then I would wander back just in time for the service to finish. It seemed to work well at the time. Amberley got to go to church, and I did not have to stay in an atmosphere that, for reasons I did not understand, seemed to internally grate and irritate me.

By now we had been home for close to a year and a half and we were in the middle of the darkest time of our life. It was not our son that was making things incredibly tough for us; it was our own internal reality. It seemed like every piece of junk that had ever taken root within us was all coming up to the surface at once. How I missed the days where I felt loved by God and enjoyed loving Him back. How I missed the days of feeling anything other than anger towards everyone. I was so wrapped up in this I could not see a way out. Every time I even thought about escaping this dark hate, it seemed to increase its stranglehold on me, suffocating me emotionally. It was killing my soul. I felt trapped. I hated everyone—especially those closest to me. I hated that no one could change our reality. I hated that no one could understand. I hated that everyone else seemed to have it good. I hated that others were happy. I hated that we could not afford food. I hated that we could not love each other. I hated myself because I could not help my son. I hated that I could not pull myself out of this downward spiral that I was falling into. The ability to love seemed like such a distant reality. It was overwhelming to even think about it.

One Sunday I was standing in church. I do not know why I did not embark on my usual dairy run that morning, but for some reason I had stayed. I was standing there in worship and I began to sob like a baby. I did not know why, but I felt something beginning to come up inside me. It was like a deep root was being pulled up within me. It gradually came up closer and closer to the surface. As it began to rise, the anger and hate began to boil up with it. I was enraged! The memories of my son suffering like he had flooded my mind. All the times we had no money to put food on the table, or petrol in the car came back to mind. The times where there was nobody around and we felt abandoned. Every one of these thoughts made me more angry and more hateful.

Suddenly it all just bubbled over and I said straight to God Himself, "I hate you!" That was all I could say, "I hate You! I hate You! I hate You!" I sat there with my nose running and tears streaming down my face. I did not know what I was expecting the Father to do in response, but I sure was not prepared for what happened next.

In that moment, I felt Him reach down, softly rub my back and gently say, "Finally, son . . . something real."

What? I thought to myself as I sat there in a crumbled heap on my knees. *God is not offended at me for saying that?!?!*

Then speaking directly to Him I asked, "You mean to tell me that You're not angry at me or offended for saying that to You?"

"Nope, not one bit," He replied in a light-hearted and slightly joyful tone.

My mind was spinning out of control. It just did not make sense. *Not only is He not angry at me,* I thought to myself, *but it sounds like He's proud of me!*

Father spoke again and said "Son, you have to understand that I have seen this all along. Even though you thought you were hiding it from Me, I could see it as clear as day. It's nothing new to Me." I could see a slight cheekiness in His eyes as He spoke. The fact that I had tried to hide something from Him seemed to make Him want to hold me tighter and burst out laughing.

I could see in that moment that this anger and hate had been at the foundation of my life all along. It was nothing new to God; He had seen it there the whole time. I realised that I had been trying to hide it behind the transparent glass wall of my heart. I thought He would be disappointed if He ever saw that in me.

I started to see all the amazing times the Father and I had shared together over the years: the miracles, the moments of love, the gatherings, the times when I was out in the bush alone with Him . . . I began to realise that He even saw this anger and hate in me back then, yet He still absolutely loved me and did not withhold Himself from me.

I realised that the year leading up to that moment had been a time of chopping off branches. When an arborist chops down a big tree, they take out the branches first and then bring the main trunk down, piece by piece. On that day, in our little church, God pulled up the final root. He uprooted the anger and hate that had been at the foundation of my whole way of living for as long as I could remember. He took me to a garden in that moment. It had been completed cleared out—every tree had been uprooted and every weed was gone. All that was left was a rich dark soil ready to be re-planted.

He said, "This is your heart."

I looked out over the empty soil with a sense of embarrassment. *Shouldn't this look more beautiful and alive?* I thought. The Father, however, looked at it like He was staring at his prized possession—a thing of beauty that needed to be admired. It was like He could see something that I couldn't.

With excitement and adventure in His voice He leaned close and whispered, "It's ready to be replanted!"

As I walked out of the little church building after

the service that morning, I felt like I was about to lift off the ground. I felt lighter than air. I was actually walking carefully because I felt like my next step was going to miss the concrete under me! I asked my wife to drive as I did not think I would be able to. I sat in the passenger seat and I realised that I had no idea who I was anymore! It was not like I had forgotten my name, or where I lived, but I had no idea who I was beyond that point. *What do I like? What do I dislike? What am I passionate about? What are my dreams? What is my purpose? What is my identity?* As weird as it sounds, being at this fresh starting point was all very exciting for me.

For over a year up to that point I had been locked in a prison of anger and had not been able to see past hate. Suddenly I was completely free of that dead weight and I was an empty garden ready to be planted with whatever the Lord wanted to grow! Previously I had been a pretty confident kind of a guy. I knew what I wanted and what I did not want. Now, I had absolutely no idea. I realised that everything I had ever been was built upon the lie of anger and hate—even the good. When that foundation was uprooted, so was everything else. I was completely empty—in a good way!—and ready for re-planting. Over the coming days and weeks I was like a little kid learning everything for the very first time!

Relationship vs. Love

Prior to our son's birth, I had been so excited at the thought that I would receive a deeper understanding of the Father's heart for His children. Once our son was born, however, I began to learn a whole lot about the Father's heart that I never expected. I came to experience His heart in ways that I would never have asked to understand, that's for sure.

I now know what it is to love someone who cannot hear my voice—not because he does not want to, but because his hearing has been robbed.

I now know what it is to love someone who cannot speak to me—not because he does not want to, but because his voice has been stolen.

I know what it is to love someone who cannot walk properly—not because he does not want to, but because his ability to walk has been under attack.

This is the Father's heart for every person on the planet. This part of His heart began to break my own. When we pray, "Break my heart for what breaks Yours," this is the part of His heart we encounter. Oh, how it breaks us in the best kind of way. It is not a brokenness that comes from sadness. It is a brokenness that is the result of overwhelming love.

My love for my son is not dependent upon how well he can hear me or speak back to me. My love for him is something that he cannot change. I love him so much and it is in that love that I long to hear his voice and for him to hear mine. I long to see him run and play because I know the joy he will find in it.

It sounds odd to say but relationship and love are two different things. His love towards us is unconditional and is not dependent on us in anyway. Relationship, however, is a two-way reality that is built upon trust and communication. My relationship with my son has its challenges because the ability for us to communicate has been severely limited. We have our own unique ways of reading each other and communicating our love towards each other. But the reality is the depth of our relationship is restricted because of the limited level of communication. At this stage I am unable to share stories with him and laugh with him. I am unable to hear what is going on in his heart and he is unable to hear what is going on in mine. Although my relationship with my son has these limitations, my love for him is absolute. I am in no way angry at him because his hearing has been robbed or because his voice has been stolen. I am not mad at him because he is unable to walk and run the way he is meant to. In fact, he holds a very special and very dear place in my heart because of the challenges he faces.

We have to understand that the Father is not angry at people simply because they do not share a relationship with Him. He is excitedly anticipating the moment when they let love in and begin their journey with Him. God's love for people is the very essence of His healing power.

Healing is God's love in action. Deliverance is God's love in action. Some people are so hurt, and their trust has been so damaged, that they simply need to see something real, something tangible—something that shows them that this love is more than just words. To the unclothed, the love of God is clothes; to the hungry, it is food to eat; to the thirsty, the love of God is water. To the homeless, it is a place to live. To the deaf person the love of God is the opening of his ears to hear; to the blind, the love of God is sight; to the lame, it is the ability to walk; to the sick, the love of God is healing. To the broken, His love is wholeness; to the lost, God's love is a home. To the mentally ill, His love is a sound mind. To the world, God's love is His Son.

His love is the answer to every problem the world could ever face, and His love is not simply a few nice words written on a page. It is a very present and very active reality!

There are no conditions on God's love. His love really is unconditional. He does not heal someone so that He can then love them; He heals them because He already loves them. Healing is the love of God in action. In other words, love is not the result of healing; healing is the result of love.

For so long we have put conditions on God's love where He did not. When He heals someone and shines His love towards them, what they choose to do with His love in no way affects His love towards them. Our response does not control His choice to love us. Nothing on our end can change the fact that He loves us unconditionally! If a person chooses not to build a relationship with Him, our Father does not simply forget about them. He turns up the heat of His fiery love and passion towards them and remains in hot pursuit. He does not love us to get love in return. He does not even love us because we need it. He loves us because it is who He is, and He will never deny who He is.

We know that God is love. So let us look at what love looks like.

> *Love is patient, love is kind. It does not envy, it does not boast, it is not proud. It does not dishonour others, it is not self-seeking, it is not easily angered, it keeps no record of wrongs. Love does not delight in evil but rejoices with the truth. It always protects, always trusts, always hopes, always perseveres.*
>
> *Love never fails.*
>
> 1 Corinthians 13:4-8, NIV

His love truly is unconditional. There are no strings attached! Relationship, however, is a different thing. We enter relationship through the doorway of love. If we want to have a deep relationship with Him, it requires that trust be built. Trust is directly proportionate to the depth that we intimately know a person.

Trust is not something where God is close-fisted, but at the same time, neither is He unwise with it. He is looking for those to whom He can entrust His deepest secrets and dreams. Trust comes as a result of intimacy. God is not simply looking for someone whom He can tell what to do; He is looking for people who understand how He thinks. Psalm 103:7 tells us that although Israel knew His acts, Moses knew His ways. Israel knew what God could do, but Moses knew why He did it.

It is a relationship of deep friendship the Father desires to share with us:

> *No longer do I call you slaves, for the slave does not know what His master is doing; but I have called you friends, for all things that I have heard from My Father I have made known to you.*
>
> John 15:15

Jesus, being the perfect representation of the Father, gives us an amazing insight into the heart of the Father in this passage. It shows that the Father is not simply looking for slaves whom He can tell what to do. He is looking for friends with whom He can share His deepest thoughts.

Psalm 25:14 says:

> *The secret of the Lord is for those who fear Him, and He will make them know His covenant.*

The word "secret" here can also be translated "counsel" or "intimacy." The counsel and the intimacy of the Lord is for those who fear Him. To fear God does not mean to be scared of Him. He does not want intimidated friends who are scared of Him. In fact, we know that perfect love casts out all fear.[1] So, the closer we get to Him who is perfect love, the more fear begins to dissolve.

So what is it to fear God in a way that allows Him to entrust us with His secrets? The word, "fear," in Psalms 25:14 means, "to be morally reverent." This means that we know and respect the way He feels about things. It means that we care about what He thinks is right and wrong. It means we value His heart. When we value God's heart, He can trust us with it.

Many people get the idea of relationship with God and the love of God mixed up. There are no conditions on God's love. Like I said, it is absolute. God the Father loves and values your heart and the heart of every person on the planet. Relationship happens when we learn to love and value His heart in return.

Heaven's Spotlight

I want to stir a hunger in you for a faith that is real. This is a faith that does not keep you at arm's length from peoples' situations, but instead, it sends you headlong into the centre of them. We need people who carry a real faith—a faith that delivers on the promises of God in every situation. We need real faith in everyday life, not just in a good healing meeting!

I come face-to-face with people nearly everyday whose situations in life are scary to even look at. It would be a lot more comfortable to ignore them, or at least keep them at a distance so that I am not impacted at the heart level. The key to maintaining a real faith is not hiding yourself from the storms of others, but rather, learning to carry peace into the centre of them. Remember, faith does not deny the mountain exists; it simply knows it can move it.

Faith at this level gets involved in peoples' lives allowing God's world to connect with theirs. It is an amazing reality that within these broken vessels (me and you) is God's kingdom which holds the answer to the overwhelming pain of those with whom we interact. I personally believe that God is looking for those He can entrust great works of healing on a scale the world has not yet seen.

I believe that depth of trust will be found in those who are not willing to stop at simply praying for people in a church meeting, or on the street, but are also willing to spend days, weeks, months, and even years, loving the one into life. This will be a people whose heart to love others will not be satisfied in a two-minute prayer that brings no change, but instead, they will be willing to serve the lowly and the afflicted. I believe it is these people that will see healing come in ways where we have up until now only dreamt about.

Not only will these ones release healing but they will become healing to the nations. In choosing to serve the afflicted, and like Jesus, lay their lives down for the sake of serving another, the Lord will also entrust to them a mantle of healing that is so tangible, that those with whom they simply spend time with will be made whole. When we think of serving, we often thinking of serving a leader, a ministry, or someone on a stage. Those are good ways to serve. But I also believe this kind of trust is going to be developed in those who are willing to serve the disabled, the afflicted, the despised—all those who face unbearable challenges. Serving with diligence and honour the unknown, the unloved, and the ones our society is trying to forget, will build within us a character that is able to carry the fullness the Father longs to pour out.

I believe the Lord wants to entrust cities and nations to those who have learned to value such individuals. Those who truly are faithful to care for the afflicted, the hurting, the forgotten, and the small, are the ones to whom the Lord will say, "Well done, faithful one. Because you have been trustworthy with these few, I will give you several cities!"[2]

These hidden generals are the greatest threat to the enemy because they are not afraid to love—even when it hurts. They are not afraid to stop and give themselves fully to serving the life of a single, lowly, unseen person, though it may cost them the stage in front of a thousand. Their priority is to be His love on the earth, not just to talk about it.

I remember waking in the middle of the night one time, and I could not get back to sleep. After lying there for a while, I decided to get up and write down some thoughts. As I was writing, I began to see something the Lord was showing me. I saw people serving the children I had been with that day. One small, 4-year-old boy in particular was unable to move his legs and wheelchair-bound. I had spent a bit of time just hanging out with this young fella on the playground. As I was with the Lord that night, I saw someone serving this young boy—just being with him, playing with him, and laughing with him. It was just the two of them—no one could see what was going on and it was not broadcast to the world in any way. But what I saw next blew me away! This person who was serving the young boy found himself standing in the spotlight of heaven's stage being watched, in awe and anticipation, by millions of witnesses in eternity. This person sacrificed an earthly stage, with all its recognition, for the lowly place of serving a young disabled boy, and in doing so, had almost accidentally found himself centre stage in heaven's most anticipated story!

Heaven's stages look vastly different to the ones here on earth. Heaven will often set up its highest platform in the lowest of places. It will set up its most magnificent stage in the presence of one unknown, afflicted, and despised person. In serving these hidden treasures, we will find ourselves standing centre stage before heaven, being applauded and made famous in eternity as God's great heroes!

End Notes

1. See 1 John 4:18.
2. Luke 19:17. See also vs. 12-27.

REFLECTION

Take a moment to reflect on your life. Ask yourself, "What heavenly stages do I stand on?" In other words, what areas of my life are seemingly insignificant here on earth, but are, in actual fact, under the spotlight of heaven?

In many cases, you will find these heavenly stages look like serving others. It could be a relationship where you are serving your spouse, children, your friend, your parents, your neighbour, a community of people—the list is endless.

Take note of these areas and the people that you are involved with. Create a deep value in your heart for these particular areas by experiencing the pleasure of the Lord towards it.

Ask yourself the following questions in regards to these heavenly stages in your life:

1. What heavenly stages can you recognise in your life right now? Are there any relationships in your life right now that you feel hold this position?

2. Are you stewarding these relationships faithfully? Is there anything you feel you should be doing to better serve this person?

3. What heavenly stages do I have a heart and passion for that I don't see in my life right now? Are there any specific people groups you have a desire to serve (i.e., the homeless, orphans, the disabled)? What age group (i.e., adults, children, teens)?

235

4. If you cannot identify any of these "heavenly stage" relationships in your life, ask yourself why. Is there a specific reason for this? Are you protecting yourself, perhaps, from these relationships? Or is it simply an area that does not come naturally to you? Is this something you can see opportunity for in your life?

You are the God
Who loves and saves us
You broke the chains
That once enslaved us
Now we are free
You've opened Heaven
Rewrote the song
The earth is singing out

"God Who Loves and Saves Us"
by Josh Klinkenberg

Activate

Healing

In this chapter, I will share how to activate the gift of healing in and through your life.

We know that life and death are in the power of the tongue. The spoken word is one of the simplest ways to release the Kingdom that is within you. Jesus spoke to the sick, the possessed, the dead, and even nature itself. When He did, no matter what the situation, it fell in line exactly with what He spoke. We are also instructed to lay hands on the sick and release the Kingdom in this way.

> *They will pick up serpents, and if they drink any deadly poison, it will not hurt them; they*

will lay hands on the sick, and they will recover.

Mark 16:18

When you understand that Christ's kingdom is within you, the laying on of hands makes sense. The spoken word, combined with the laying on of hands, has become the most common way I release healing to those in need.

There are three parts I like to keep in mind when releasing healing to the sick. These are not the only way to release healing; they are simply guidelines that have helped me.

1. Command

The first part is to command the pain to go in the authority we have in the name of Jesus. There are times where we need to speak to the condition directly and command it to leave.

Jesus clearly told us how to address the mountain we are facing.

> *And Jesus answered and said to them, "Truly I say to you, if you have faith and do not doubt, you will not only do what was done to the fig tree, but even if you say to this mountain, 'Be taken up and cast into the sea,' it will happen."*

Matthew 21:21

Sometimes I speak specifically to the part of the body that is affected by illness; other times I speak to the person's body as a whole.

2. Release Healing

Secondly, I intentionally release healing to the person

afflicted. This simply means I release exactly what the person needs through speaking it out. Not only do I speak life over that person, but I also command their body to be healed. We see throughout the gospels that Jesus was very direct in releasing the command to people's bodies to be healed. This is a prophetic declaration that releases exactly what the person needs from heaven. When you speak out the command, "Be healed!", you are releasing the very substance of healing into the atmosphere of that person enabling them to come into alignment with that reality.

3. Test It Out

The third element is that I ask the person to do something they were not able to do before. Just as Jesus told the crippled man to pick up his mat and walk, and to the man with the withered arm He asked him to stretch out his hand, so too we need to ask the person we are praying for to do something that was previously difficult, painful, or impossible. It is often with this act that healing comes. Why? Because it is where their faith is activated.

We need to understand that when we give a command for healing, we actually release the ability for that command to be fulfilled. When Jesus commanded the man with the withered arm to stretch out his hand, He released the ability with the virtue of heaven for him to do that very thing. The healing command of Jesus enabled him to actually stretch out his hand. With that act, he discovered he was healed. In the same way, numerous disabled people that Jesus commanded to rise up from their bed and walk found that they were able to do so. It was the same when Jesus commanded Lazarus to come out of his tomb, and the same for the little girl who had died that Jesus commanded, "Get up!"[1] He released a command which contained power within it to see that exact command become reality. That is the power of life God has put inside of you and me.

Remember, this is a simple guideline to activate your own faith to see people healed in the name of Jesus. I have seen many people healed outside of the use of this "structure" of prayer. I have seen people healed who were not even expecting it at all. Others have been healed when someone simply touched them and spoke the word, "Heal!" And still others Jesus has healed through one of His children simply looking at the person. So this is by no means a formula that needs to be followed exactly. It is simply a tool following the pattern we see Jesus using in the gospels.

We often read of Jesus "binding" the disease or the spirit behind the disease. Then, by speaking the word, or by laying His hands on the person, healing would be released to them. Following this, Jesus would ask or even command them to do something they previously could not.

> *Jesus said to him, "Get up, pick up your pallet and walk." Immediately the man became well, and picked up his pallet and began to walk.*
>
> John 5:8-9

We also know that even though Jesus operated like this regularly, it was not a rigid formula that restricted Him. One time, He put mud on a blind man's eyes made from His own spit. Another time He healed people by simply saying, "Your faith has made you well!" So there is no set formula. Hearing the voice of the Father by His Spirit, and following His lead, should always be our highest priority.

For those who are just starting out and need some

encouragement to be activated in praying for healing, I like to recommend these tools as a guide. And for the sake of simplicity, I have put the three steps together in the order that I most often use them.

> 1. **Bind** the sickness and **command** it to leave.
>
> 2. **Release** healing.
>
> 3. **Ask** the person to do what they could not do before. (Remember, this is often where they see the manifestation of the healing you just released to them.)

I really love to see people get creative with the gifts of the Spirit. I believe the way that it has always been done has got us this far; but I also know it is time for something new. Don't be afraid to explore new tools and find new ways of releasing His kingdom. In fact, I encourage you to regularly try new ideas. Spend time dreaming with God about new, fun ways that you can partner with Him to release the Kingdom.

With that said, I only share the above "1-2-3-step" guide as a way to get people activated with courage in the healing gift. But even Jesus Himself did things different each time, so too we can expect the Holy Spirit will add the unique "seasoning" that is only found in your relationship with Him as you develop more courage in releasing healing to those around you. Without a doubt, you will be blessed and encouraged with each and every person you pray for as you embark on this awesome adventure!

Awareness

Let me add this before you "do" anything: awareness

of the Lord Himself is the key. It is the key to moving in any of the gifts that the Holy Spirit gives us. To be "aware" of Him and His presence—aware of how close, active, and able He is—will be the key to seeing the Kingdom flow freely and powerfully through you. So before you do anything, the first step is to stop and become aware of Him. Allow yourself to know the reality of how close He is. Breathe Him in and get the sense that He fills the very air around you. Know that He clothes you with His Spirit:

In Him we live, move and exist.

Acts 17:28

Let His presence be your reality. The more you practice becoming aware of Him, the quicker and easier this reality is realised. I urge you to spend considerable time "practicing" the presence of God by allowing sufficient time for Him to come and just be with you so you learn what it is like to simply be in Him. Let it become more than something that you have to "step into." Live there.

From this place of awareness, begin to think of Scriptures where Jesus commanded us to heal the sick, raise the dead, cleanse the lepers, and cast out demons.[2]

Meditate on these. Realise that when Jesus released this command, He also released the ability, power, and virtue for it to happen in its entirety.

Look at your hands. Realise the miracles He has already placed in those hands: see the healings, deliverances, and the signs and wonders. Realise that by your spoken words, life will be released: life that will see peoples' bodies made completely whole; life that will see peoples' situations brought into submission to heaven's destiny for them; life that will see God's glory cover the earth.

From this place of awareness, a communion with the Holy Spirit begins to emerge. You will flow freely, powerfully, and in harmony with the Spirit of God. It is from this place of awareness that we see Jesus move and release His healing power to the degree that "all were healed." Jesus saw what His Father was doing, and He simply partnered with it as He commanded the person in need right into alignment with heaven.

End Notes

1. See Mark 5:41.
2. Matt. 10:8.

PRAYER EXAMPLE

I learn a lot from hearing and seeing people in action. So, in an attempt to show you what this would look like in a "real" life situation, I have put an example of how I would generally go about releasing healing to someone. I say "generally" because the Holy Spirit is incredibly creative, and from the place of awareness, the encounter with the afflicted person can be completely different. Of course, this example will look different in varying situations.

If I was to minister to someone who had some sort of knee problem, I would apply the three simple steps I outlined in this chapter. It might look something like this:

Pain, I bind you and command you to loose your hold and leave this body now.

Knee, be healed. I release movement and freedom to the joints, ligaments, tendons, and muscles.

Knee receive health and wholeness.

That would be it! Then I would ask the person to do something they were not able to do before.

Try to move your knee now. [Encourage them to move their leg.]

Remember, this step is very important. This is where their faith is activated following the command you released in the name of the Lord. Then ask them:

Do you feel any pain?

The person would have one of three results: they would either be better, the same, or worse.

If the person is better, I would ask:

Would you say you feel 100% better, 80% better, 50% better, or something less?

If they answer 100%, then thank the Lord and bless them! If they are anything less than 100%, I would simply repeat the same healing prayer again and command that body part in need to be healed, whilst at the same time **thanking the Lord for what He has done.** Remember, the way to bring increase in the Kingdom is to thank Him for the little you have already received and don't focus on what you do not have. For example, when Jesus needed to feed the 5,000, what did He do with the small lunch He had? He thanked the Father for that which He had, and in doing so, the increase was released to feed the whole crowd—with leftovers, even!

If the person replies that they feel "the same," I repeat the same process again, realizing that the pain or condition has to shift because of the authority He has given us. Jesus gave us authority over sickness; it is that simple. I have done this very thing several times over people before, seeing only the slightest shift in their health; but it has to shift, nonetheless!

I have stood in front of a room full of people— sometimes hundreds—on many occasions and have released healing with no visible result. Undeterred, I simply pray and command again.

Still nothing.

I remember one time I was instructing the congregation that as believers, we all have the ability to release healing.

So, I had each of them pray for someone around them who needed healing. I led them through once, and asked for people to test it out and do something they could not do before. Not one person was healed. I simply led people in repeating the release of healing through prayer. We told those receiving prayer to do something they could not do before. Again nothing. This went on five times! As you can imagine, it was like there was a giant vacuum at the back of the hall sucking every last bit of faith out of the room.

Finally, after the fifth time releasing healing, someone waved their hand at me and announced, "I'm healed!"

Then, as healing hit this one person, faith flooded back in the room and suddenly, it began to spread. It began with one, then there were two, then four, then a dozen, and on it went. Literally, an explosion of healing hit the room and people were being healed just as we were pointing out that others had been healed.

Why did it happen this way? Because faith is more contagious than unbelief.

I cannot tell you how common this scenario is. If we had stopped after releasing healing once, we would probably have only ever seen a half a dozen people healed. But because we pushed through and stubbornly believed God at His Word, we have seen hundreds healed and set free. This leads those who were healed into a radical encounter with the Father's love.

I also mentioned that one of the three results could be that the person you prayed for responds that their condition is worse. If that is the case, I have found that it is usually due to a demonic spirit afflicting them directly. This spirit is simply "playing up" because of the presence of God that you are releasing over the person. It is important to note that this does not mean the person is possessed by a demon, it simply means they have had a demonic assignment on their life that has manifested in the condition they have. In this case, bind the demonic spirit and command it to loose its hold and go. Then release healing into that person's body once again.

It is worth pointing out that demons do not respond to volume; they respond to the authority given to you in Jesus. So we do not need to be loud or dramatic when dealing with a manifestation of demonic spirits. Don't give them the pleasure of attention. Just bind them, tell them to leave, and be done with them.

When we are ministering at a healing meeting we will often train the congregation to release healing themselves. When we do this en mass, I will ask the people receiving healing prayer to test it out and wave at me if they are better. Sometimes after the first round of prayer we see a handful healed; sometimes we see none. This does not bother me because I know we are going to release another round of prayer. Then I tell the congregation, "Wave at me if there is no change and you're still the same." Usually this is the largest group of people the first time round. And finally, I ask those who are feeling worse to wave at me. Oftentimes a couple of people will wave at me indicating they are feeling worse off than they did before receiving prayer. They usually have a look of disappointment on their faces like they have done something wrong, or a look that says, "I knew this was too good to be true. . . ."

But with excitement I instruct those praying for them to slightly alter the way they are praying and to break off the assignment of the enemy on their life. I tell them to rebuke the demonic attack that has been aimed at them and to declare freedom and a hedge of protection in the Holy Spirit. Almost every time, these people who were feeling worse begin to see immediate improvement after this is done. I love seeing that look of disappointment dissolve as faith and hope begin to rise!

249

The King who is over all
Through You and by You
All things were made
Son of the Most High God
The ocean is but a teardrop
Against Your love

"The Greatest King"
by Josh Klinkenberg

CHAPTER

13

Pursuing

Breakthrough

When we decide to go after breakthrough in a long-term condition or in something that does not seem to be shifting, our trust in the Lord can take a real knock. I have seen many people, and even entire churches, hit with a crippling discouragement when they actively go after breakthrough in a specific person or area where no manifested change is seen. It can be very hard not to be bitter and disappointed in God when we choose to come together as a body to fast and pray for a specific person who is suffering and yet not see any breakthrough whatsoever in them.

I remember going after my son's healing and getting so angry and disappointed in God. I remember feeling so let down, and I really struggled to trust Him in a number of other areas because of it. So what do we do in these situations? How do we maintain a healthy heart and relationship with the Lord whilst at the same time going after breakthrough in the areas that are not easily moved?

It is important to start at the root. The issue here is a relational one: between us and our heavenly Father. When we pray for someone to be healed—multiple times even—yet see no breakthrough come, our disappointment can cause us to shy away from pursuing breakthrough in that area. We may feel things like, "I didn't have enough faith," or "I just don't have the gift of healing."

In situations where there is a lack of breakthrough, we can often make the mistake of becoming passive in our approach towards healing, when all we really need is a bit of clarity and wisdom into what is actually going on. What we need to realise is that ultimately it is our trust towards the Lord that is being challenged. When we are involved in a situation where we are not seeing the breakthrough we are asking for, we can feel like the Lord has broken our trust because He hasn't come through in the way we thought He said He would come through. This is a totally legitimate feeling. Although it is self-inflicted, it is still legitimate, and we need to acknowledge that we feel this way.

When we are faced with situations where we are not seeing breakthrough, we can begin to question ourselves and God; we feel inadequate, or we feel like God is distant. This only leads to one place: anger, frustration, and discouragement. When we begin to realise that the real issue is that our trust towards Him is being challenged, we can then start to live in a way that protects our trust in Him and that provides a nurturing and healthy place for that trust to grow.

I see so many believers taken out and robbed of seeing further breakthrough because of this kind of discouragement. What I have realised in my own journey is that discouragement of this type is self-inflicted as we unknowingly sabotage and violate our own trust towards God. I have since learnt to live in a new way that provides a healthy place for my trust in God to grow and mature whilst continuing on the journey of pursuing breakthrough in these "stubborn" areas.

So let's look at how we can live in such a way where we can contend for breakthrough in the area we are not seeing it and stay in faith and healthy connection with the Father.

Firstly, we have to recognise our needs in the relationship with the Lord. Every relationship has needs that facilitate the health and depth of that relationship. While this may be weird to think about, our relationship with the Lord is no different. We have needs invested in our relationship with the Lord which benefit us when we are aware of them. When it comes to faith, healing, the gifts of the Spirit, and the supernatural in general, we as human beings have been created with a common need: to see answered prayer.

To grasp this properly we first need to understand what needs are. Needs are not demands or conditions that we have on a relationship in order for it to work. Needs are the things that we are aware of which enable us to feel loved, seen, and accepted by the other person. Needs should facilitate and develop the health of the relationship. So when we talk about a need to see answered prayer, we are acknowledging that the experience of answered prayer causes us to experience a fresh sense of love and acceptance from the Father. We are not saying that we feel hated, unseen, and disowned when we don't see answered prayer take place. Our identity

253

is not in the answered prayer. But those who have seen and experienced answered prayer will know what it feels like in those moments: a fresh experience of His love and goodness floods us.

God's Love Language

Answered prayer is one of the love languages we share with the Lord. For example, I know my wife loves me and I know that she cares for me deeply. But when I see that in action, it still makes me feel loved and accepted by her in a fresh way. It wasn't that I didn't feel loved beforehand; it's just that I am touched again by the manifestation of her love for me. To make someone feel loved does not require that they first feel unloved. Love is ever-increasing. It is alive, and grows to new heights every single day!

So, to acknowledge that we feel loved, seen, and accepted when we experience answered prayer never implies that we felt unloved; it simply acknowledges the reality that our love can grow. And just as a plant needs water to grow, we have need of the continued experience of answered prayer. The reason this can be hard for us to hear and acknowledge at times is because we think that meeting our needs is all on the Lord's end and that we are putting requirements on Him. This is definitely not the case. When we recognise a need in us, it is not so that we can create obligations for Him to meet; it is so that we can position ourselves in a healthy way where that need can be met consistently. It is to empower us to position ourselves to feel loved, seen and accepted.

To Know Him

The Lord has created us in such a way that we have an inherent need to see answered prayer. We need to see the impossible take place. We need to see the reality of our partnership and communion with Him manifest through us into the world around us. It is a part of our journey of getting to know Him for who He really is. When He reveals one of His names to us, it is because He is inviting us to experience that part of who He is. When He says He is Provider, we then have a need to experience that in order to truly know Him as Provider. It does not mean we need to be poor in order to see His provision; it simply means that whether rich or poor, I have a need to experience Him as Provider because that is who He is. And, until I meet that side of Him, I will only ever know about Him, when what He really desires is that I would experience Him.

Likewise, if He says He is Healer, then I need to experience Him as Healer in order to know that side of Him. When He calls Himself Healer, I have an open invitation to experience Him as Healer. And I won't truly know Him as Healer until I do. This does not mean I need to be sick in order to encounter this aspect of His personage. God's character as Healer is not dependent upon sickness because He can reveal Himself to a person as Healer even in the absence of sickness. But the fact still stands: we have a need to experience Him as Healer because we are drawn to know all of Him. To live in a way where we are continually exposed to, and experiencing answered prayer, enables us to begin to truly know and experience Him.

"Who Do You Say That I Am?"

When it comes to healing, the Lord is asking us the same question He asked of His disciples, "Who do you say I am?" We need to get to the place in our hearts where we can wholeheartedly say, "I know You are Healer." This only comes through experiencing answered prayer. When you stand before the disabled, the lame, the sick, the dying, He is asking you this question, "Who do you say I am?" It is then that we need a history with God that we can stand upon and say, "I know You are Healer!" This history is only developed through experiencing continued answered prayer.

We have a need to experience the manifestation of the partnership and communion we share with Him.

When we do not see regular answers to prayer, we begin to lack a vital part of our relationship with the Father and can easily fall prey to disappointment and discouragement.

Who do you say He is?

One of the greatest keys to maintaining faith in the midst of pursuing a breakthrough is to be careful not to put "all our eggs in one basket." By this I mean when we choose to go after a breakthrough that is not moving quickly, we can put all of our focus and attention into that one thing, and it means that we have everything going out and nothing coming back in. When this happens our need to see and experience answered prayer is not met because we have positioned ourselves unwisely. And when this need is not met, we begin to flirt with disappointment.

One of the best things we can do is to live in a way where we have multiple streams of encouragement. Like any good business owner knows, you want to have multiple streams of income in place so that if one stream runs dry, the business does not die. When a business becomes completely dependent upon one job, it places itself in a very risky position. And even though it might work out once, it is not a sustainable, or wise way to continue to operate. So it is with our walk in healing and faith. When we realise that God has created us with a need to see and experience answered prayer, we can begin to position ourselves in a way where that need is continually met, all the while continuing to pursue breakthrough in areas that we are not yet seeing a shift.

We need to have multiple areas of breakthrough in our life. For instance, my wife and I are going after breakthrough in our son. It didn't take me long, however, before I was discouraged and disappointed. And from that point, my trust towards the Father began to deteriorate. This all changed when I re-positioned myself so that I didn't have all my eggs in the one basket. Now I position myself in such a way where I am regularly exposed to answered prayer, allowing that need in my relationship with the Father to be met. I do this by seeing breakthrough in many other areas. This could be as simple as praying for other people who have a need of healing.

It is important for us to understand that we need to protect and regularly invest in our trust in the Lord. When we understand this, we can begin to strategically strengthen and nurture our trust towards the Lord. When we see breakthrough in an area, we can then run headlong into anything and everything that we see needing breakthrough. And although this can turn over some results, it can also be really damaging to our trust towards God. The damage we cause to our trust is self-inflicted and is only the result of a lack of wisdom. The Father never breaks our trust, but we can often position ourselves in a way that allows our trust to be broken. It seems like a paradox, but it is true. Oftentimes we pick battles that are noble, but when we put "all our eggs in that basket," they are damaging to our trust towards the Father. Why? Because our trust towards Him is built in us by seeing and experiencing answered prayer. When we recognise the need He has put in us to see and experience answered prayer, we are then able to position ourselves in a way where we can see that need met, resulting in our trust being strengthened. From there we are able to pursue breakthrough in the more "stubborn" areas whilst protecting our trust towards the Father.

We need to allow our trust in Him to grow. When I received healing from hay fever many years ago I decided I would go after healing for everyone I came across with hay fever. Without knowing it, I was allowing my trust in Him to grow and mature by continuing to see answered prayer in an area that I was actively seeing breakthrough in. This allowed my trust in Him to strengthen and mature to the point that I was able to begin to move outside that area of immediate breakthrough to explore new ground without it causing damage to my trust towards the Father as Healer.

Stewarding our breakthrough is equally as important as receiving it in the first place. I love seeing people who have a fiery passion to see breakthrough come to long-term disabilities, diseases and conditions. But I am also aware of how many people have been dealt a "knockout blow" because they have not learnt to create multiple streams of encouragement in their life. We need to see breakthrough in syndromes, disabilities, problems from birth, and other long-term conditions. And the way we are going to remain healthy in the possessing of this "Promised Land" is by positioning ourselves to see continued breakthrough and answered prayer along the way.

We can achieve this by continuing to intentionally operate in areas where we have developed a strong faith. Continue to actively move in the areas that you have received breakthrough. Experience answered prayer by seeing pain leave people's bodies. Allow the areas of breakthrough in your life to strengthen and bless your trust in the Father as Healer while you go after the giants in your life that are too stubborn to leave quickly.

If you are a part of a church body that is going after

healing in people from your church family, keep going, and have an expectation to see the full breakthrough that is promised to you! But along the way, I encourage you to stay active in seeing breakthrough in other areas as you walk this journey together as a church family. Never allow yourself to have "all your eggs in the one basket." This is not the best way to serve the person you are contending to see breakthrough in. You serve them best by cultivating a culture that is regularly exposed to the miraculous, allowing the reality of Jesus as Healer to manifest and to be a constant reminder that He is good and that He can be trusted.

The Maker of Heaven
Chased me down
Your love is relentless
Your love now my crown
So I'll spend my days
Pouring out my heart
On You
Singing, "I love You"

"I Love You"
by Josh Klinkenberg

14

Two Final

Treasures

I want to end this book by sharing two important thoughts that the Lord has taught me over the course of our journey together in releasing healing. The first is to understand the difference between a process of healing and an instant miracle. There are a couple of significant things that will help us—especially in the long term—to appreciate the difference between the two.

This is not necessarily something that changes the way I pray or the way I speak about healing. As with everything in this book, it is not for the sake of an argument, but rather to encourage you to remain in faith. Let me explain what I mean.

The Healing Process

Healing can be an instant miracle or it can take place over a period of time. For example, many people who are healed of some type of internal cancer receive healing, but then a process kicks into effect. In the moment they receive their healing the cancer dies, and their body now has a new powerful environment to do what it is created to do: regenerate the cells that restore health. Oftentimes, during this process, people may feel worse over a period of several days, or even weeks, as their body rejects and attempts to eliminate the dead cancerous cells present in their body. After several days or weeks, the cancerous growth exits the body and that person begins to feel well again.

In the case when an instant miracle takes place, the person with cancer receives prayer and the cancerous tumour or growth completely disappears in an instant with no trace whatsoever. It simply no longer exists in their body. From this point on, the healed person's natural immune system kicks back in and restores their body to complete health, and/or the Lord also completely restores them at the moment.

Although both are equally valuable and equally miraculous, it is still important that we understand these various ways in which healing takes place. Why? Because if we do not, we can fall into the trap of devaluing a way that the Lord chooses to operate. The reason I say this is because in many cases, a person receives healing, and then in a day or so, they start to feel worse than they did before they were prayed for. In that moment the person may start to believe the lie, "I must not be healed," and in doing so opens the door for sickness to take hold of them once again. What happened?

Whatever we agree with we empower. If we agree with the enemy, the father of lies, we empower the enemy and his lies. If we agree with truth, we empower truth. When we make a declaration, "I am not healed," we are, in effect, handing over our inheritance of healing and wholeness to the enemy, while at the same time giving him permission to make that statement our reality.

Sometimes when a person experiences familiar symptoms from an illness they were healed from, people have labeled this as "the devil trying to steal the healing." In many cases this is absolutely true. But what often happens at first is the body is simply reacting physically to a massive change that has taken place. The devil very rarely attacks us when we are feeling strong because he knows the only authority he has is what we give him. He prefers to wait until we are weak, and then he strikes, often with much success.

When Jesus was in the desert for forty days, the devil did not come to him right away. He waited until Jesus was at His very weakest.

Yes, the enemy tries to steal our healing. What can often happen at the beginning of our healing is this: as our bodies are reacting to a physiological change that healing brought, the process of being healed can cause us to feel weak, sore, sickly, tired and a variety of other symptoms. And this is precisely the time when the enemy tries to step in.

The body is complex, and as it is in transition from sickness to health, we often experience a crisis of symptoms. The bodily systems are attempting to remove toxic waste and that can also make us feel very "sick." Those who have done long-term food fasts understand this phenomenon. As the body works hard to remove

263

years of toxins and poisons buried deep within tissues and organs, it also releases a variety of sick-symptoms that can be misunderstood as illness. This is simply the body's natural purifying process working hard to flush out all that should not be there in order that the body can shift back into its intended state of health. It is the way God designed our bodies to function.

When we have been healed and the body is making its adjustments, we need to be aware of the temptation to doubt the Word of the Lord, because this is just when the enemy steps in—when we feel weak.

I also think it is worth mentioning that this belief system of the devil coming in and stealing the healing is often rooted in an age-old lie: the devil is very present and the Father is very distant. But the reality is that our heavenly Father does not heal our body and then stand far off. He does not give the devil access to His children— those He loves so dearly. The devil is not able to simply walk up and take the gift that He gave us. Only *we* have the power to hand it over to him. Selah.

I once saw a man healed who must have been in his 70s. He had suffered from paralysis in his left arm for over a decade. As we prayed and he began to test out the healing, this man noticed feeling come back into his arm and hand. But because he had not used that arm in so long, the muscles had no strength whatsoever. He could not even lift it up off his leg as he sat in his chair. There were a few stages in his healing that he could have easily chosen to believe satan's lie, which would have allowed the paralysis to set back in.

Firstly, he had received healing, but did not have immediate use of his arm after a decade of immobility. He could have chosen to see this and say, "I am not healed."

But he had the spiritual maturity to discern the process of his healing that needed to happen over time. His arm had been restored, and the ability to move it had returned, but because the muscles were too weak at that moment, he knew it was going to take time to strengthen them to full mobility and range of motion.

Secondly, anyone who has ever done an exercise workout will know that when you work your muscles for the first time you feel the results for the next three or four days! I remember the first time I went to the gym with my brother in-law. He got me doing one of his advanced chest workouts. Men being men, I pushed myself as hard as he did and tried to keep up with him, even though he had been going to the gym for months already. I was tired when I went to bed that night, but felt okay. The next morning was another story. When I tried to move, the muscles in my chest screamed at me with a burst of excruciating pain. When I finally managed to roll out of bed, I felt as if Mike Tyson himself had unleashed a full twelve rounds of fury on my chest during my sleep. The worst part was that it got even more severe as the days went on. After the third day, the pain slowly started to subside, but it still took a week to fully recover and another week for full movement to be restored.

The elderly gentleman whose arm was healed faced a similar challenge immediately after his healing. Many people with conditions that involve muscles or movement can feel very sore and restricted the days immediately after receiving healing. It is very important that we realise what is going on in our body so we do not open the door for the original affliction to return because we gave up and believed the lie that we were not actually healed. What is often happening is the muscles are simply responding to being worked in a way that they have not experienced in a long time. The muscles are growing and strength is building. And that takes time.

Our bodies were created in such a phenomenal way that they actually have the ability to heal. When we are attacked by sickness or disease, our immune system fights it off and then repairs the damage. There are certain conditions, however, where our immune system is unable to defend itself. Healing, in these cases, is where the Lord removes the root problem that caused our health to deteriorate, and in doing so, He gives our bodies a chance to do the job He created them to do. After we see healing manifest in our body, a good question to ask the Lord is, "Is there anything I can do to partner with You in sustaining and stewarding my health?" Without a doubt God will bring resources to us and show us a good path to maintain a healthy body.

In our passion and desire to see instant results, we must be careful not to discredit or devalue this form of healing that takes place over a period of time. I have found it is quite common for people to come away from healing meetings and find that they are gradually getting better and better until they are completely healed and whole again. As I said, I always pray with faith and with an expectancy for an instant miracle to take place, and we see these happen regularly. We love it! But at the same time, I have come to also appreciate how many people receive healing gradually over subsequent days and weeks. This is God's healing way too! We must learn to bless, value, and acknowledge all the life-giving ways God chooses to heal.

With this beautiful gift of God, let us remember that the Lord commanded us to heal the sick. As to how that happens, well, it can look very different each and every time.

Preach the Kingdom

The second treasure I want to leave you with has to do with preaching the Kingdom. Healing is the result of the Kingdom coming to earth. Preaching the Kingdom is why we were sent and what He commissioned us to do. Jesus tells us in John 20:21:

> As the Father has sent Me, I also send you.

So, if we can understand the purpose of why Jesus was sent, we can find the purpose with which He sent us.

> But He said to them, "I must preach the kingdom of God to the other cities also, for **I was sent for this purpose.**"
>
> Luke 4:43, emphasis added

His purpose was to preach the Kingdom. When we also take on this primary purpose, we align ourselves with Him. I am a musician by trade and love nothing more than to listen to harmonies formed by two or more notes complementing each other. When I hear a good harmony I love to turn up the volume on my stereo so I can feel the resonance of the relationship between those two notes. Jesus released a specific sound; He was playing a specific note. His sound was the Kingdom; the result was people got healed.

We get this extraordinary privilege to harmonise His sound with ours. When two notes harmonise with each other, they are accentuated because of their relationship. It is like a chemical reaction between two musical notes. You can have two chemicals, which in and of themselves are powerful. But when you put them together they become explosive! That is what good harmony is. It is two notes coming together to create such an explosive resonance that the whole room begins to vibrate.

When we bring our message into harmony with Jesus' message we find that suddenly it is like the volume was turned up. The sound that Jesus released has reverberated throughout time from when He first proclaimed, "The Kingdom of God is here!" Let us determine not to be a dissonant harmony to that note so that when people hear it, they have to turn it down. Rather, let us be a sound filled with beauty, resonating in harmony with the sound of Christ. In this musical dance we become an explosion of life on the earth—a sound that finds favour with God and with man. We will find that not only will people want to hear us, they will actually turn the volume up, meaning, we will have great influence into their lives.

I noticed a dramatic change in our ministry when we started preaching the Kingdom. I used to preach healing which is a good thing. Nonetheless, it is not what we were sent to preach. That is what we were sent to *do*. We saw some miracles in doing this but never the kind of breakthrough that we desired. So when God showed me that I was preaching healing when He wanted me to preach the Kingdom, I realised we had been focusing people on the wrong thing.

Healing is a sign that is designed to point people to the Kingdom. When we started preaching and proclaiming the Kingdom, we saw healing begin to explode. We became a harmony to His sound and the explosion of life began!

It makes sense when you begin to look at the Scriptures and see that whenever the Kingdom was proclaimed, the sick were healed.

*Jesus was going throughout all Galilee, teaching in their synagogues and **proclaiming the gospel of the kingdom**, and healing every* *kind of disease and every kind of sickness among the people.*

Matthew 4:23, emphasis added

If we want to sound like Jesus, we will preach the Kingdom with power. When we declare like Jesus, "The Kingdom . . . is here," we are acknowledging a reality that Jesus already established. And with that awareness, this reality is manifested.

Luke 9:2 is an awesome prophetic picture of what it looks like to be sent by Jesus.

He [Jesus] *sent them out to **proclaim** the kingdom of God and to **perform** healing.*

Luke 9:2, emphasis added

It is a lot simpler than many of us were originally led to believe.

*And as you go, **preach, saying, "The kingdom of heaven is at hand."** Heal the sick, raise the dead, cleanse the lepers, cast out demons. Freely you received, freely give.*

Matthew 10:7-8, emphasis added

Our message is the Kingdom and its King. Our method is healing, deliverance, and resurrection life. Let us not replace the message with the method or we will be introducing people to a tool instead of the Toolmaker. Oftentimes we are preaching the things we are meant to be "doing." Jesus did not preach much at all about healing the sick. He just healed them, and He commanded us to go and do the same! Let's make our primary message the Kingdom!

We are carriers of the Kingdom. We must not settle for just carrying one of its fruits; we carry the whole thing!

I have seen a lot of zealous people sacrifice love in the name of their cause. Keeping the Kingdom as the focus prevents us from the temptation of merely trying to prove a sign that points to the Kingdom and releases us instead to present the full Kingdom itself.

As I have said, and will continue to say, my goal with this book is not to give another theological argument in favour of healing. That would be a waste of my time and yours. But rather, I want to give you an impartation of faith in your inner being where you would come to a complete rest in His Spirit knowing that His heart is to heal all who need His touch.

The intention of this book is to enable believers, like yourself, to move in power for the sake of releasing His love! You see within the pages of this book that I have a special love for this particular gift of healing. But even so, I always keep in mind that healing is a sign that points to the greatest reality of all: Jesus is alive, and He longs to share a relationship with every single person!

I pray that we in this generation would be able to pass on to our children a faith that is pure, powerful, and undefiled by unbelief. May our children not have to fight the same battles that we spent so many years fighting. I pray we would hand them a Promised Land inheritance instead of a war that we should have won. I pray that we would be a people who, through intimacy and deep relationship with the Father, would be able to give our children a rich inheritance and understanding in the art of healing.

Amen.

ASSIGNMENT 7

Your final assignment is a stretching one!

❖ *For this assignment, you are going to see one person healed every day for a week.*

Starting from the next Monday that comes around, you are going to release the love of God through healing to someone everyday for seven days. The person you release healing to can be anyone, anywhere. You might find them in your home, at work, at school, down the street, as your driving, at the supermarket, in town, or even at the mailbox.

It doesn't matter who and it doesn't matter where, the goal is to actively minister healing to at least one person everyday for a week.

If you happen to minister to two or more people on one day, that is great! It doesn't, however, mean that the next day you get a "day off." For this assignment you are required to minister to at least one person for each of the seven days.[1]

Things to remember

❖ *Your goal is for your target to experience that they are loved by God.*

❖ *At times through the week you might*

have to position yourself intentionally to achieve this assignment.

✤ *Write down the testimonies in your miracle journal.*

✤ *Have fun! Enjoy the adventure!*

End Note

1. If you have a testimony that has come as a result of reading *The Art Of Healing* or completing one of the activations in this book, I would personally love to hear from you! Email your testimony to: josh@inflameworshipschool.com and put the word "Testimony" in the subject line. I look forward to hearing from you.

—Josh

ABOUT THE AUTHOR,

JOSH KLINKENBERG AND HIS WIFE AMBERLEY are the directors of InFlame Ministries. They live in Tauranga, New Zealand with their three children, Elijah, Rain, and Indie.

Josh travels throughout New Zealand and further afield. His life and ministry is marked by signs, wonders and miracles, especially in the area of physical healing. Working with numerous churches, Josh trains and activates them into the supernatural.

InFlame began as a worship school on a small island off the coast of New Zealand and has quickly become a national training ground for creatives across all streams in the body of Christ. Now known as InFlame Academy, Josh and Amberley have a heart to see the body of Christ living in intimacy and power.

As a worship leader, speaker, producer, author, and musician, Josh and Amberley have a heart to see the indigenous cultures redeemed, restored, and released into their full expression within the Kingdom. As well as being Sounds of the Nations NZ directors, Josh and Amberley are Jesus Culture Music artists and have released their EP, "Our Love," through Jesus Culture Music.

RESOURCES

Josh and Amberley Klinkenberg are the founding directors of InFlame Ministries which began as a small worship school on an island off the coast of New Zealand. Today InFlame has grown into a multifaceted ministry that serves the nation and the nations in stepping into their Kingdom identity with power. InFlame has several branches to it including InFlame Studios, InFlame Publishing House, InFlame Music and the recently launched InFlame Academy, which is online training for those who want to explore the depths of the Father's heart and their relationship with Him.

InFlame Academy

InFlame Academy is an online spiritual education environment where students are empowered and equipped to move in the fullness of the Kingdom life. It caters to those who want to explore the depths of the Father's heart and their relationship with Him. InFlame Academy offers training to both individuals and groups in a number of different areas: worship, healing, the prophetic, hearing

God's voice, songwriting, prophetic painting, and many other courses.

InFlame Academy gives the student access to courses, events, live-streams, and skills-based training in an all-in-one online location that can be accessed anytime, from anywhere. At InFlame Academy, students receive Kingdom training that facilitates intimacy with the Father whilst also providing an environment to connect with others who share a heart for the fullness of the Kingdom life. This custom-built online platform makes it incredibly simple to connect with fellow students and tutors alike.

Contact InFlame Ministries for more information:

www.inflameministries.com

info@inflameministries.com

Miracles In Aotearoa New Zealand

Testimonies from the Life and Ministry of R. Weston Carryer

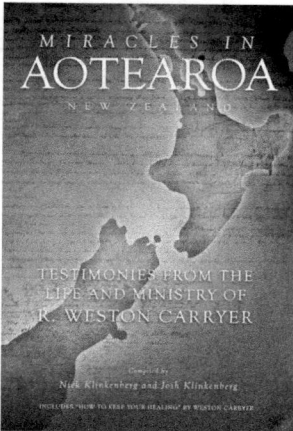

Weston Carryer is one of New Zealand's most notable healing evangelists. His life and story show the incredible love and willingness God has for His people. This book is filled with stirring testimonies of those healed through the ministry of Weston Carryer.

It also includes, "Keeping Your Healing," written by Weston Carryer. The original booklet was distributed to hundreds as they experienced the power of God heal their body. *Miracles In Aotearoa New Zealand* will encourage you to trust God for the impossible.

Book   659 pages

Our Love

EP by Josh & Amberley Klinkenberg

"Our Love" is a three-song introductory EP that came about in a partnership between Josh and Amberley and Jesus Culture Music. Recorded and released in 2013, these songs come out of Josh and Amberley's journey with the Father through the good times and the bad. The title, "Our Love," reflects the genuine heart behind these songs—to release a sound of love and praise in all things. "Our Love" can be purchased through iTunes and most other major music outlets. The full-length album is due out in the near future.

For more music from the Klinkenberg's visit:

www.klinkenbergmusic.com

The books

Art of Healing: A Journey Into the Miraculous

and

Miracles in Aotearoa New Zealand

are available for sale at:

www.inflameministries.com